TEACHER'S PET PUBLICATIONS

LITPLAN TEACHER PACK
for
Julie of the Wolves
based on the book by
Jean Craighead George

Written by
Mary B. Collins

© 1996 Teacher's Pet Publications
All Rights Reserved

This **LitPlan** for Jean Craighead George's
Julie of the Wolves
has been brought to you by Teacher's Pet Publications, Inc.

Copyright Teacher's Pet Publications 1996
11504 Hammock Point
Berlin MD 21811

Only the student materials in this unit plan (such as worksheets,
study questions, and tests) may be reproduced multiple times
for use in the purchaser's classroom.

For any additional copyright questions,
contact Teacher's Pet Publications.

www.tpet.com

TABLE OF CONTENTS - *Julie of the Wolves*

Introduction	5
Unit Objectives	7
Reading Assignment Sheet	8
Unit Outline	9
Study Questions (Short Answer)	13
Quiz/Study Questions (Multiple Choice)	24
Pre-reading Vocabulary Worksheets	43
Lesson One (Introductory Lesson)	57
Nonfiction Assignment Sheet	59
Oral Reading Evaluation Form	61
Writing Assignment 1	64
Writing Assignment 2	71
Writing Assignment 3	75
Writing Evaluation Form	72
Vocabulary Review Activities	67
Extra Writing Assignments/Discussion ?s	69
Unit Review Activities	77
Unit Tests	81
Unit Resource Materials	117
Vocabulary Resource Materials	133

A FEW NOTES ABOUT THE AUTHOR
JEAN CRAIGHEAD GEORGE

Jean Craighead was born in Washington D.C. in the year 1919. Jean and her twin brothers, John and Frank, grew up in a family with a love for the outdoors. She attended Pennsylvania State University and graduated with a B.A. in 1941.

A few years later she married John George with whom she had three children, a girl and two boys. Although in the beginning they co-authored several works, probably the most noteworthy being *Dipper of Copper Creek*, the couple gradually grew apart and eventually divorced in 1963.

Jean Craighead George spent the early part of her career as a reporter for the International News Service and the *Washington Post and Times Herald*. From 1960-1968 she was a continuing education teacher in Chappaqua, New York, and from 1969-1980 she worked as a staff writer and roving editor for *Reader's Digest*.

Since the publication of *Dipper of Copper Creek* in 1959, Ms. George has written a long list of children's books as well as nonfiction, all relating in some way to nature. She is not only a prolific writer, but a writer of quality, as well: the list of awards she has won for her writing is almost as long as the list of titles she has written.

The books for which she has won the most awards are *My Side of the Mountain* and *Julie of the Wolves*, which were also both Newbery Medal winners.

INTRODUCTION - *Julie of the Wolves*

This unit has been designed to develop students' reading, writing, thinking, and language skills through exercises and activities related to *Julie of the Wolves* by Jean Craighead George. It includes eighteen lessons, supported by extra resource materials.

The **introductory lesson** introduces students to Alaska. Following the introductory activity, students are given a transition to explain how the activity relates to the book they are about to read. Following the transition, students are given the materials they will be using during the unit. At the end of the lesson, students begin the pre-reading work for the first reading assignment.

The **reading assignments** are approximately thirty pages each; some are a little shorter while others are a little longer. Students have approximately 15 minutes of pre-reading work to do prior to each reading assignment. This pre-reading work involves reviewing the study questions for the assignment and doing some vocabulary work for 8 to 10 vocabulary words they will encounter in their reading.

The **study guide questions** are fact-based questions; students can find the answers to these questions right in the text. These questions come in two formats: short answer or multiple choice. The best use of these materials is probably to use the short answer version of the questions as study guides for students (since answers will be more complete), and to use the multiple choice version for occasional quizzes. It might be a good idea to make transparencies of your answer keys for the overhead projector.

The **vocabulary work** is intended to enrich students' vocabularies as well as to aid in the students' understanding of the book. Prior to each reading assignment, students will complete a three-part worksheet for approximately 8 to 10 vocabulary words in the upcoming reading assignment. Part I draws on students' general knowledge of the words, asking students to write down what they think the words mean. Part II adds the element of context to aid the student by giving the sentence in which the word appears in the text. Students are then to write down what they think the words mean based on the words' usage. Part III nails down the definitions of the words by having students find the words in a dictionary and write down the definitions appropriate for the contextual uses of the words. Students should then have an understanding of the words when they meet them in the text.

After each reading assignment, students will go back and formulate answers for the study guide questions. Discussion of these questions serves as a **review** of the most important events and ideas presented in the reading assignments.

After students complete reading the work, there is a **vocabulary review** lesson which pulls together all of the fragmented vocabulary lists for the reading assignments and gives students a review of all of the words they have studied.

Following the vocabulary review, a lesson is devoted to the **extra discussion questions/writing assignments**. These questions focus on interpretation, critical analysis and personal response, employing a variety of thinking skills and adding to the students' understanding of the novel.

The **group activity** which follows the discussion questions has students working in small groups to plan a camping trip.

There are three **writing assignments** in this unit, each with the purpose of informing, persuading, or having students express personal opinions. The first assignment is to inform: students write a letter from Julie to Amy in which Julie tells Amy about her life in Alaska. The second assignment is to persuade: students write a letter from Amy to Julie persuading her to come to San Francisco to live. The third assignment is to give students a chance to simply express their own opinions and be creative: following the group activity, planning a camping trip, students write a narrative about their imaginary trip.

In addition, there is a **nonfiction reading assignment**. Students are required to read a piece of nonfiction related in some way to *Julie of the Wolves*. After reading their nonfiction pieces, students will fill out a worksheet on which they answer questions regarding facts, interpretation, criticism, and personal opinions. During one class period, students make **oral presentations** about the nonfiction pieces they have read. This not only exposes all students to a wealth of information, it also gives students the opportunity to practice **public speaking**.

The **review lesson** pulls together all of the aspects of the unit. The teacher is given four or five choices of activities or games to use which all serve the same basic function of reviewing all of the information presented in the unit.

The **unit test** comes in two formats: multiple choice or short answer. As a convenience, two different tests for each format have been included. There is also an advanced short answer unit test for higher level students.

There are additional **support materials** included with this unit. The **unit resource** section includes suggestions for an in-class library, crossword and word search puzzles related to the novel, and extra vocabulary worksheets. There is a list of **bulletin board ideas** which gives the teacher suggestions for bulletin boards to go along with this unit. In addition, there is a list of **extra class activities** the teacher could choose from to enhance the unit or as a substitution for an exercise the teacher might feel is inappropriate for his/her class. Student materials may be reproduced for use in the teacher's classroom without infringement of copyrights.

UNIT OBJECTIVES - *Julie of the Wolves*

1. Through reading *Julie of the Wolves*, students will study the importance of adapting to the changes in one's life and environment.

2. Students will demonstrate their understanding of the text on four levels: factual, interpretive, critical and personal.

3. Students will review survival skills.

4. Students will learn about Alaska and the Eskimos.

5. Students will plan a camping trip to exercise their skills in organization and logical thinking.

6. Students will be given the opportunity to practice reading aloud and silently to improve their skills in each area.

7. Students will answer questions to demonstrate their knowledge and understanding of the main events and characters in *Julie of the Wolves* as they relate to the author's theme development.

8. Students will enrich their vocabularies and improve their understanding of the novel through the vocabulary lessons prepared for use in conjunction with the novel.

9. The writing assignments in this unit are geared to several purposes:
    a. To have students demonstrate their abilities to inform, to persuade, or to express their own personal ideas
        Note: Students will demonstrate ability to write effectively to <u>inform</u> by developing and organizing facts to convey information. Students will demonstrate the ability to write effectively to <u>persuade</u> by selecting and organizing relevant information, establishing an argumentative purpose, and by designing an appropriate strategy for an identified audience. Students will demonstrate the ability to write effectively to <u>express personal ideas</u> by selecting a form and its appropriate elements.
    b. To check the students' reading comprehension
    c. To make students think about the ideas presented by the novel
    d. To encourage logical thinking
    e. To provide an opportunity to practice good grammar and improve students' use of the English language.

READING ASSIGNMENT SHEET - *Julie of the Wolves*

Date Assigned	Assignment	Completion Date
	I: Beginning to "fur carpeted house and lay down."	
	I: "Miyax's eyes fluttered" to the end of I	
	Part II	
	III: Beginning to "They were crying for Amaroq."	
	III: "The sun went down on November tenth" to the end	

UNIT OUTLINE - *Julie of the Wolves*

1 Introduction PV Assignment 1	2 Read Assignment 1 PV Assignment 2	3 Read Assignment 2 PV Assignment 3	4 Study ?s Part I Read Assignment 3	5 Study ?s Part II Writing Assignment 1 PV Assignment 4
6 Read Assignment 4 PVR Assignment 5	7 Guest Speaker	8 Study ?s Part III Vocabulary	9 Extra ?s	10 Writing Assignment 2
11 Group Activity	12 Group Activity	13 Writing Assignment 3	14 Nonfiction Reports	15 Review
16 Test				

Key: P = Preview Study Questions   V = Prereading Vocabulary Work   R = Read

STUDY GUIDE QUESTIONS

SHORT ANSWER STUDY GUIDE QUESTIONS - *Julie of the Wolves*

Part I
Reading Assignment 1

1. Why was Miyax afraid?
2. What did Miyax want to tell the wolf?
3. What happened to Miyax's father?
4. What did Miyax hope to share with the wolves?
5. Why did Miyax choose the black wolf to help her?
6. How did the author describe Miyax?
7. Why did Miyax speak half in English and half Eskimo when she said, "Amaroq, Daya, wolf, my friend"?
8. How long will it be before the sun sets?
9. Why did Miyax not take a compass?
10. Why do creatures of the Arctic tend toward compactness?
11. To where did Miyax intend to walk?
12. What did Miyax want to do at Point Hope?
13. What is the wolf signal for "lie down"?
14. What did Amaroq do when Miyax laid down?
15. What was the negative effect of the hour of the lemmings' being over?
16. Why didn't the abundance of the caribou help Miyax?
17. What do gussaks say about wolves?
18. What did Miyax call the mother wolf? Why didn't she call her Martha?
19. What did Miyax name the grey wolf?
20. Why did Miyax name the last wolf Jello?
21. What was Eskimo wealth?
22. How did full grown wolves express their love for their leader?
23. How did wolf puppies express their love for their leader?
24. What did Miyax call the brave black puppy?
25. Why did Eskimos place their clothes in bladder bags at night?
26. Why did Amaroq tolerate Miyax?
27. When Miyax saw herself in the water, what did she look like?
28. What was keeping the wolf pups fat and healthy?
29. Why was Jello excited by Miyax's humble voice?
30. What kind of partners are Miyax and Kapu?
31. What did Miyax use instead of wood to make a fire?

Julie Short Answer Study Questions Page 2

Reading Assignment 2

32. What are "white-outs"?
33. What had the wind told Amaroq?
34. Why did the two-ended tunnel worry Miyax?
35. Why did Miyax make a trail when she went hunting?
36. Why didn't Miyax catch the owl?
37. Who won the fight between Amaroq and Jello?
38. What did Silver do when Miyax drank her milk?
39. How did Miyax know the direction to Fairbanks?
40. How could Miyax tell it was almost autumn?
41. Why does every Eskimo family have a deep cellar in the ice?
42. How did Kapu react to the Eskimo food Miyax gave him?
43. How long does the Arctic night last?
44. How did Miyax know it was August 24th?
45. How did Miyax scare Jello away from her food?

Part II

Reading Assignment 3

1. How old was Miyax when her mother died?
2. Where did Kapugen go when his wife died?
3. Who was Naka?
4. Why did the hunters return the bladders to the seals?
5. What was the whale like to Miyax.
6. Why did Miyax not like summers at the seal camp as much as the winters?
7. What was Miyax's English name?
8. How did Miyax react when Kapugen called her Julie?
9. Who came when Kapugen was making Miyax's coat?
10. What important things did Aunt Martha tell Kapugen?
11. How could Miyax get away from Aunt Martha if she wanted to?
12. What happened to Kapugen?
13. Identify Mr. Pollock.
14. Why didn't Aunt Martha like Judith?
15. What did Miyax think of Daniel upon meeting him?
16. What is Nusan's job?
17. What problem did Naka have?
18. What was Kapugen's saying about fear?
19. What did Pearl give Miyax?
20. What was Pearl to tell Nusan? Why?
21. Where was Miyax going?

Julie Short Answer Study Questions Page 3

Part III
Reading Assignment 4
1. What did Miyax get from the pups' den?
2. Who took Miyax's food?
3. Why couldn't Miyax strike Jello when he surrendered?
4. What from her pack did Miyax most want to find?
5. How did Jello die?
6. What did Miyax use to make some equipment she needed?
7. What did Kapu bring Miyax?
8. What would guide Miyax to Point Hope?
9. What did the fact that she saw a skua tell Miyax?
10. What are bounties and what did they encourage?
11. What did the oil drum mark?
12. Identify Tornait.
13. Who was Amaroq training to be the new leader of the pack?
14. Why did Miyax hide in the oil drum?
15. What happened to Amaroq?

Reading Assignment 5
16. What problem did Amaroq's death cause for the wolf pack?
17. Why did Miyax move her pack to the river?
18. Where did Miyax decide to live?
19. Who were Miyax's visitors?
20. Where were hunter and his family from?
21. Who was Atik's teacher?
22. What about Kangik pleased Miyax?
23. Who did Miyax find in Kangik, and what did she discover about his lifestyle?
24. Why did Miyax leave her father?
25. To what realization does Miyax come?
26. What are we made to believe at the end of the story?

ANSWER KEY: SHORT ANSWER STUDY GUIDE QUESTIONS - *Julie of the Wolves*

Part I

1. Why was Miyax afraid?
   She was afraid because she was lost.

2. What did Miyax want to tell the wolf?
   She wanted to tell him that she was starving, and she wanted to ask for food.

3. What happened to Miyax's father?
   He paddled his kayak into the Bering Sea and disappeared.

4. What did Miyax hope to share with the wolves?
   She hoped to share food with them.

5. Why did Miyax choose the black wolf to help her?
   She chose him because he appeared to have wisdom and to be the leader.

6. How did the author describe Miyax?
   She described Miyax as being the "classic Eskimo beauty."

7. Why did Miyax speak half in English and half Eskimo when she said, "Amaroq, Daya, wolf, my friend"?
   She hoped the wolf would understand her sentiments in one of the languages she knew.

8. How long will it be before the sun sets?
   It will be a whole month before the sun sets.

9. Why did Miyax not take a compass?
   She didn't take one because she had always had the birds and plants to lead the way and to tell the direction.

10. Why do creatures of the Arctic tend toward compactness?
    A compact design conserves heat.

11. To where did Miyax intend to walk?
    She intended to walk to Point Hope.

12. What did Miyax want to do at Point Hope?
    She wanted to meet the ship, the North Star, and earn her way to San Francisco where her pen pal, Amy, lived.

13. What is the wolf signal for "lie down"?
    Bared teeth and narrow eyes say "lie down.

14. What did Amaroq do when Miyax laid down?
    He wagged his tail.

15. What was the negative effect of the hour of the lemmings' being over?
    The animals that preyed on the lemmings were also gone.

16. Why didn't the abundance of the caribou help Miyax?
    She had no way to kill one.

17. What do gussaks say about wolves?
    They say that wolves eat people.

18. What did Miyax call the mother wolf? Why didn't she call her Martha?
    She called her Silver because she was much too beautiful to call Martha.

19. What did Miyax name the grey wolf?
    She called him Nails.

20. Why did Miyax name the last wolf Jello?
    She called him Jello because when he quivered, he reminded her of jello.

21. What was Eskimo wealth?
    Intelligence, fearlessness and love made Eskimo wealth.

22. How did full grown wolves express their love for their leader?
    They bit him under the chin.

23. How did wolf puppies express their love for their leader?
    They lay down in front of him, wag their tails and stare at him in "pure adoration."

24. What did Miyax call the brave black puppy?
    She named him Kapugen after her father.

25. Why did Eskimos place their clothes in bladder bags at night?
    The bags kept them dry, for dampness could mean death in the Arctic.

26. Why did Amaroq tolerate Miyax?
    She was a sad child with no gun.

27. When Miyax saw herself in the water, what did she look like?
    She looked like the "gussak girls" with hollowed cheeks, not an Eskimo rounded face.

28. What was keeping the wolf pups fat and healthy?
    Meat from the "belly basket," partially digested food from the adults, kept them healthy.

29. Why was Jello excited by Miyax's humble voice?
    He was so used to being bossed around that he was surprised someone could respect him.

30. What kind of partners are Miyax and Kapu?
    They are "joking-serious" partners.

31. What did Miyax use instead of wood to make a fire?
    She used dry grass and lichens.

32. What are "white-outs"?
    A white-out happens when the snow is so thick in the air that one cannot see through it.

33. What had the wind told Amaroq?
    The wind told Amaroq a herd of caribou was nearby.

34. Why did the two-ended tunnel worry Miyax?
    It told her that this was only a temporary shelter for the wolves and that after a few weeks they would leave.

35. Why did Miyax make a trail when she went hunting?
    The tundra was without natural landmarks, and she needed to be able to find her way back to her camp.

36. Why didn't Miyax catch the owl?
    He could have hurt her with his claws and beak.

37. Who won the fight between Amaroq and Jello?
    Amaroq won.

38. What did Silver do when Miyax drank her milk?
    She grabbed Miyax on the shoulder with her teeth and wouldn't let go.

39. How did Miyax know the direction to Fairbanks?
    She saw a plane flying overhead, and she figured out that it was probably going to Fairbanks.

40. How could Miyax tell it was almost autumn?
    The sun was at the edge of the horizon.

41. Why does every Eskimo family have a deep cellar in the ice?
    They use the cellar as a big freezer to preserve food.

42. How did Kapu react to the Eskimo food Miyax gave him?
    He loved it and ate it up.

43. How long does the Arctic night last?
    It lasts 66 days.

44. How did Miyax know it was August 24th?
    On that date the sun goes below the horizon for just one hour.

45. How did Miyax scare Jello away from her food?
    She threatened him with her knife.

Part II
1. How old was Miyax when her mother died?
    She was four.

2. Where did Kapugen go when his wife died?
    He went to a seal camp to live.

3. Who was Naka?
    Naka was Kapugen's serious partner.

4. Why did the hunters return the bladders to the seals?
    They believed that the bladders held the spirits of the seals. They returned the bladders so the spirits could enter the bodies of the newborn seals and keep them safe until harvest time.

5. What was the whale like to Miyax.
    It seemed like a mountain.

6. Why did Miyax not like summers at the seal camp as much as the winters?
    Kapugen was always busy in the summers; she could spend more time with him in the winters.

7. What was Miyax's English name?
    Her English name was Julie.

8. How did Miyax react when Kapugen called her Julie?
   She became very angry and said, "I am Eskimo, not a gussak!"

9. Who came when Kapugen was making Miyax's coat?
   Miyax's Aunt Martha came.

10. What important things did Aunt Martha tell Kapugen?
    She told him that he had to go to war and that Miyax had to go to school.

11. How could Miyax get away from Aunt Martha if she wanted to?
    If she doesn't like living with Aunt Martha, Miyax may marry Daniel, Naka's son, when she is thirteen.

12. What happened to Kapugen?
    He went seal hunting in his kayak and never returned.

13. Identify Mr. Pollock.
    He was Miyax's pen pal's father.

14. Why didn't Aunt Martha like Judith?
    Judith misbehaves and talks back to her parents and doesn't closely follow the old Eskimo ways.

15. What did Miyax think of Daniel upon meeting him?
    She was disappointed because there was something wrong with him.

16. What is Nusan's job?
    She makes parkas and mittens for the tourists.

17. What problem did Naka have?
    He drank too much and abused his wife.

18. What was Kapugen's saying about fear?
    He said that when fear seizes, you should change what you are doing because you are doing something wrong.

19. What did Pearl give Miyax?
    She gave her food, a sleeping skin and a ground cloth.

20. What was Pearl to tell Nusan? Why?
    She was to tell Nusan that she saw Julie going out on the ice so Nusan would think Julie drowned and wouldn't look for her very long.

21. Where was Miyax going?
    She was going to San Francisco to see her pen pal, Amy Pollock.

Part III
1. What did Miyax get from the pups' den?
    She got a bone with teeth marks on it to make into a comb, and she got a second bone to make into a weapon.

2. Who took Miyax's food?
    Jello did it.

3. Why couldn't Miyax strike Jello when he surrendered?
    She couldn't strike a coward.

4. What from her pack did Miyax most want to find?
    She wanted to find her ulo, needles and matches.

5. How did Jello die?
    Amaroq fought with him and killed him because he had done something bad to Miyax.

6. What did Miyax use to make some equipment she needed?
    She used frozen grass and frozen leather.

7. What did Kapu bring Miyax?
    Kapu brought a leg of caribou for Miyax.

8. What would guide Miyax to Point Hope?
    She would use the North Star.

9. What did the fact that she saw a skua tell Miyax?
    It told her that she was getting closer to the ocean because skuas only live in the coastal Arctic.

10. What are bounties and what did they encourage?
    A bounty is a sum of money offered to anyone who brings in a certain kind of animal. Bounties encouraged killing for money instead of for need.

11. What did the oil drum mark?
    It marked the beginning of civilization.

12. Identify Tornait.
    Tornait was a little plover (bird) Miyax found and kept as a pet.

13. Who was Amaroq training to be the new leader of the pack?
    He was training Kapu.

14. Why did Miyax hide in the oil drum?
    Hunters were nearby in a plane. She thought they might mistake her for an animal and shoot her, so she hid in the drum for safety.

15. What happened to Amaroq?
    The hunters in the plane shot and killed him and never even came back for his body.

16. What problem did Amaroq's death cause for the wolf pack?
    Without their leader, they were starving.

17. Why did Miyax move her pack to the river?
    There were more animals for them to find to eat at the river.

18. Where did Miyax decide to live?
    She decided to live on the tundra, leading an old-fashioned Eskimo's life.

19. Who were Miyax's visitors?
    A hunter and his wife and child happened upon Miyax's home.

20. Where were hunter and his family from?
    They lived in Kangik.

21. Who was Atik's teacher?
    Kapugen was his teacher.

22. What about Kangik pleased Miyax?
    She liked the fact that it mostly looked like an old-fashioned Eskimo dog-sled village.

23. Who did Miyax find in Kangik, and what did she discover about his lifestyle?
    She found Kapugen, her father. At first she was pleased because his house looked just like their house at the hunting camp, but when she discovered that he had a wife and that he had adopted many of the modern ways of man, she was disappointed.

24. Why did Miyax leave her father?
    The father she remembered was dead to her; he had changed. She wanted the old life, which he could no longer offer her.

25. To what realization does Miyax come?
    She realizes that "the hour of the wolf and the Eskimo is over."

26. What are we made to believe at the end of the story?
    Julie returns to her father and learns to adapt to the more modern culture, accepting that the old ways are pretty much gone.

MULTIPLE CHOICE STUDY GUIDE/QUIZ QUESTIONS - *Julie of the Wolves*

Part I

1. Why was Miyax afraid?
    a. The wolves attacked her.
    b. She didn't have anything with which to make fire.
    c. Her feet got wet and she was afraid she'd freeze.
    d. She was lost.

2. What did Miyax want to tell the wolf?
    a. I'm starving; could I have food?
    b. Which way should I go?
    c. Are there any other people out here?
    d. Are you the leader of the pack?

3. What happened to Miyax's father?
    a. He got lost on a hunting trip.
    b. He died of old age.
    c. He paddled his kayak into the Bering Sea and disappeared.
    d. He had a sledding accident.

4. What did Miyax hope to share with the wolves?
    a. Shelter
    b. Food
    c. Survival techniques
    d. Her kispuck

5. Why did Miyax choose the black wolf to help her?
    a. He appeared to be smart and the leader.
    b. He appeared to be the most friendly.
    c. He was the most handsome.
    d. She picked him at random.

6. How did the author describe Miyax?
    a. "Tomboy-ish"
    b. "Pretty but rugged"
    c. "Classic Eskimo beauty"
    d. "Healthy and natural"

Julie of the Wolves Multiple Choice Study Guide/Quiz Questions Page 2

7. Why did Miyax speak half in English and half Eskimo when she said, "Amaroq, Daya, wolf, my friend"?
   a. She was delirious.
   b. Since she was going to San Francisco, she wanted to practice English.
   c. She naturally spoke both languages.
   d. She was hoping he would understand some part of the two languages she knew.

8. How long will it be before the sun sets?
   a. A month
   b. A week
   c. Six weeks
   d. Two weeks

9. Why did Miyax not take a compass?
   a. She forgot it.
   b. She had always used birds and plants to tell the direction.
   c. She thought she knew the way by herself.
   d. She didn't own one and couldn't find one to buy.

10. Why do creatures of the Arctic tend toward compactness?
    a. It increases the sensitivity of their senses.
    b. They eat less food that way.
    c. A compact design conserves heat.
    d. It makes them better fighters.

11. To where did Miyax intend to walk?
    a. Point Hope
    b. San Francisco
    c. Nunivak Island
    d. Barrow, Alaska

12. What did Miyax want to do at Point Hope?
    a. Meet Amy
    b. Meet the North Star
    c. Meet Mr. Pollack
    d. Resupply

Julie of the Wolves Multiple Choice Study Guide/Quiz Questions Page 3

13. What is the wolf signal for "lie down"?
    a. Bared teeth and a tail wag
    b. Crouch down and look down
    c. A nip under the chin
    d. Bared teeth and narrow eyes

14. What did Amaroq do when Miyax decided to lie down?
    a. Bared his teeth
    b. Nipped her chin
    c. Wagged his tail
    d. Walked away

15. What was the negative effect of the hour of the lemmings' being over?
    a. The animals that preyed on the lemmings were also gone.
    b. Darkness would soon come.
    c. The heavy snows would soon come.
    d. Miyax would have no fuel.

16. Why didn't the abundance of the caribou help Miyax?
    a. They attracted more predators to the area.
    b. She had to be careful that they didn't trample her camp.
    c. She had no way to kill one.
    d. They made her trail difficult to follow.

17. What do gussaks say about wolves?
    a. They are enchanted.
    b. They eat people.
    c. They are as friendly as dogs.
    d. They're sneaky.

18. What did Miyax call the mother wolf?
    a. Martha
    b. Amaroq
    c. Silver
    d. Nails

Julie of the Wolves Multiple Choice Study Guide/Quiz Questions Page 4

19. What did Miyax name the grey wolf?
    a. Jello
    b. Nails
    c. Amaroq
    d. Silver

20. What did Miyax name the wolf that quivered?
    a. Jello
    b. Nails
    c. Amaroq
    d. Silver

21. What was Eskimo wealth?
    a. Intelligence, fearlessness and love
    b. The natural resources under the frozen tundra
    c. The natural beauty of the land
    d. Their rich traditions and heritage

22. What did Miyax call the brave black puppy?
    a. Jello
    b. Kapugen
    c. Amaroq
    d. Nails

23. Why did Eskimos place their clothes in bladder bags at night?
    a. To keep them dry
    b. To keep them warm
    c. To keep them clean
    d. To wash them

24. Why did Amaroq tolerate Miyax?
    a. She fed him regularly.
    b. She gave him a warm place to sleep.
    c. She was a child with no gun and therefore no threat.
    d. She helped him against his enemies.

Julie of the Wolves Multiple Choice Study Guide/Quiz Questions Page 5

25. When Miyax saw herself in the water, what did she look like?
    a. An old woman
    b. A gussak girl
    c. An Eskimo girl
    d. A wolf

26. What was keeping the wolf pups fat and healthy?
    a. They were eating lichens.
    b. The adults brought home fresh meat for them.
    c. Meat from the "belly baskets" of the adults
    d. Miyax fed them.

27. What did Miyax use instead of wood to make a fire?
    a. Bushes
    b. Old clothing
    c. Caribous manure
    d. Dry grass and lichens

28. What are "white-outs"?
    a. The underbellies of caribou
    b. One has been in the snowy wilderness so long that one begins to forget things.
    c. The snow covered lairs of the wolves
    d. The snow is so thick in the air one cannot see through it.

29. Why did Miyax make a trail when she went hunting?
    a. To be able to find her way back to camp
    b. So the wolves could find her
    c. She couldn't help but make a trail as she walked in the powdery snow.
    d. So if other people would come along, they could find her.

30. Why didn't Miyax catch the owl?
    a. She made the wrong kind of trap.
    b. She was too slow.
    c. He could have hurt her with his sharp claws and beak.
    d. He was too beautiful to kill.

Julie of the Wolves Multiple Choice Study Guide/Quiz Questions Page 6

31. What did Silver do when Miyax drank her milk?
    a. She rolled over on her back.
    b. She grabbed Miyax on the shoulder and wouldn't let go.
    c. She growled and barred her teeth.
    d. She nudged Miyax with her nose.

32. How did Miyax know the direction to Fairbanks?
    a. She saw the skyline of the city on the horizon.
    b. She saw a plane flying over and assumed it was going to Fairbanks.
    c. She calculated the direction based on the location of the North Star.
    d. She used her maps.

33. How could Miyax tell it was almost autumn?
    a. The sun was at the edge of the horizon.
    b. The caribou were leaving.
    c. The snow falls were more frequent.
    d. The lemmings had returned.

34. For what are Eskimo cellars used?
    a. As extra living space
    b. As garages
    c. As freezers for food storage
    d. As playrooms for children

35. How did Kapu react to the Eskimo food Miyax gave him?
    a. He ate it but threw it up later.
    b. He loved it and ate it up.
    c. He would not eat it.
    d. He buried it.

36. How long does the Arctic night last?
    a. Three months
    b. One month
    c. 47 days
    d. 66 days

Julie of the Wolves Multiple Choice Study Guide/Quiz Questions Page 7

37. How did Miyax scare Jello away from her food?
    a. Threatened him with her knife
    b. Brought Amaroq over
    c. Waved fire at him
    d. Threw a pan at him

Julie of the Wolves Multiple Choice Study Guide/Quiz Questions Page 8

Part II

1. How old was Miyax when her mother died?
   a. Newborn
   b. 4
   c. 10
   d. 12

2. Where did Kapugen go when his wife died?
   a. To a seal camp
   b. To Fairbanks
   c. To Point Hope
   d. To his parents' home

3. Who was Naka?
   a. Kapugen's serious partner
   b. Miyax's husband-to-be
   c. Miyax's brother
   d. Kapugen's brother/partner

4. Why did the hunters return the bladders to the seals?
   a. So they could be used again
   b. No particular reason; they just did
   c. So they wouldn't be wasted
   d. So the spirits could enter the bodies of the newborn seals

5. Why did Miyax not like summers at the seal camp as much as the winters?
   a. She liked the dog races that were held in the winter.
   b. There was more to do in the winter.
   c. Kapugen was too busy to spend time with her in the summer.
   d. Summers were too rainy and dreary; at least in the winter everything was covered with a blanket of beautiful white snow.

6. How did Miyax react when Kapugen called her Julie?
   a. She didn't care.
   b. She got angry.
   c. She preferred to be called Julie.
   d. She winked at him.

Julie of the Wolves Multiple Choice Study Guide/Quiz Questions Page 9

7. Who came when Kapugen was making Miyax's coat?
    a. Aunt Martha
    b. Naka
    c. Miyax
    d. Charlie Edwards

8. What thing did Aunt Martha not tell Kapugen?
    a. He had to go to war.
    b. Aunt Martha was going to stay indefinitely.
    c. Miyax had to go to school.
    d. None of the above

9. How could Miyax get away from Aunt Martha if she wanted to?
    a. She could go work for Nusan.
    b. She could spend her vacations with her father.
    c. She could board at school.
    d. She could marry Daniel.

10. What happened to Kapugen?
    a. He went to war, returned and sent for Miyax.
    b. He went to war but wrote often.
    c. He left in his kayak and was never heard from again.
    d. He got killed at war.

11. Identify Mr. Pollock.
    a. He was Nusan's father.
    b. He was the father of Miyax's pen pal.
    c. He brought the news of Kapugen's death.
    d. He was Kapugen's serious partner.

12. Why didn't Aunt Martha like Judith?
    a. She misbehaves.
    b. She's sassy.
    c. She doesn't follow the old Eskimo ways.
    d. All of the above

Julie of the Wolves Multiple Choice Study Guide/Quiz Questions Page 10

13. What did Miyax think of Daniel upon meeting him?
    a. She was disappointed.
    b. She fell instantly in love with him.
    c. She liked him well enough and though he'd make a good husband.
    d. She thought he was a slob.

14. What is Nusan's job?
    a. She is a homemaker.
    b. She sews for the village people.
    c. She makes parkas and mittens for tourists.
    d. She dries animal skins.

15. What problem did Naka have?
    a. He didn't have enough money to pay his debts.
    b. He drank too much.
    c. He was frustrated because he wanted more education but couldn't get it.
    d. He promised more goods than he could deliver.

16. What was Kapugen's saying about fear?
    a. When fear seizes, change what you are doing because you are doing something wrong.
    b. If you are afraid, close your eyes and think a happy thought.
    c. Rational thought conquers fear.
    d. Fear is an enemy only in your mind.

17. What did Pearl give Miyax?
    a. Food, a sleeping skin and a ground cloth
    b. A parka and mittens
    c. Food and an ulo
    d. A sleeping skin, an ulo and a parka

18. What was Pearl to tell Nusan? Why?
    a. She saw Julie headed back to Aunt Martha's house.
    b. She saw Julie headed towards Judith's house.
    c. She saw Julie going out on the ice.
    d. She saw Julie trying to kill herself.

Julie of the Wolves Multiple Choice Study Guide/Quiz Questions Page 11

19. Where was Miyax going?
   a. Fairbanks
   b. Nunivak Island
   c. Alaska
   d. San Francisco

Julie of the Wolves Multiple Choice Study Guide/Quiz Questions Page 12

Part III
1. What did Miyax get from the pups' den?
    a. Bones
    b. Food
    c. A pup
    d. Rocks

2. Who took Miyax's food?
    a. Silver
    b. Jello
    c. Amaroq
    d. Kapugen

3. Why couldn't Miyax strike Jello when he surrendered?
    a. He would have torn her apart in anger.
    b. He moved too quickly.
    c. She couldn't strike a coward.
    d. She couldn't reach him.

4. What from her pack did Miyax most want to find?
    a. Her bladder and ground cloth
    b. Food
    c. Her parka
    d. Her ulo, needles and matches

5. How did Jello die?
    a. Hunters killed him.
    b. Miyax killed him.
    c. Amaroq killed him.
    d. Kapugen killed him.

6. What did Miyax use to make some equipment she needed?
    a. Frozen grass and frozen leather
    b. Jello's bones and hide
    c. Wood
    d. Caribou antlers

Julie of the Wolves Multiple Choice Study Guide/Quiz Questions Page 13

7. What did Kapu bring Miyax?
    a. Her ulo
    b. A leg of caribou
    c. Bones to make into a comb and a knife
    d. Jello's carcass

8. What would guide Miyax to Point Hope?
    a. Her compass
    b. The North Star
    c. The caribou trails
    d. The wolves

9. What did the fact that she saw a skua tell Miyax?
    a. Caribou were near.
    b. Other people had recently been there.
    c. Spring had come.
    d. She was getting closer to the ocean.

10. What did bounties encourage?
    a. Fighting among the Eskimos
    b. Farmers
    c. Settlers
    d. Killing for money instead of need

11. What did the oil drum mark?
    a. Aa trail to Point Hope
    b. The path of a river under the ice
    c. The beginning of civilization
    d. An emergency food stash

12. Identify Tornait.
    a. Miyax's pet bird
    b. One of the wolves
    c. A hunter Miyax met
    d. The wife of a hunter Miyax met

Julie of the Wolves Multiple Choice Study Guide/Quiz Questions Page 14

13. Who was Amaroq training to be the new leader of the pack?
    a. Miyax
    b. Kapu
    c. Silver
    d. Zit

14. Why did Miyax hide in the oil drum?
    a. To keep warm
    b. For safety from hunters
    c. For safety from wild animals
    d. To get out of the weather

15. What happened to Amaroq?
    a. He drowned after falling through thin ice.
    b. Kapu killed him.
    c. Hunters killed him.
    d. He starved to death.

16. What problem did Amaroq's death cause for the wolf pack?
    a. They were all going their separate ways.
    b. They were fighting among themselves and killed each other off.
    c. They weren't sleeping and were becoming vicious.
    d. They were starving without a leader.

17. Why did Miyax move her pack to the river?
    a. There were no hunters at the river.
    b. There were more animals to kill for food at the river.
    c. The pack needed fresh water.
    d. Miyax wanted to follow the river to Point Hope.

18. Where did Miyax decide to live?
    a. On the tundra
    b. San Francisco
    c. Point Hope
    d. Fairbanks

Julie of the Wolves Multiple Choice Study Guide/Quiz Questions Page 15

19. Who were Miyax's visitors?
    a. Two caribou
    b. Kapu and Silver
    c. A man, his wife and their child
    d. Ulo and Kispuck

20. Where were hunter and his family from?
    a. Atik
    b. Fairbanks
    c. Point Hope
    d. Kangik

21. Who was Atik's teacher?
    a. Naka
    b. Kapugen
    c. Daniel
    d. Miyax

22. What about Kangik pleased Miyax?
    a. It had running hot water; she was dying for a hot bath.
    b. It was clean and modern.
    c. It looked like an old-fashioned Eskimo village.
    d. It had a place where she could get good food.

23. Who did Miyax find in Kangik?
    a. Kapugen
    b. Her father
    c. Charlie Edwards
    d. All of the above

24. Why did Miyax leave her father?
    a. The father she had remembered was dead to her.
    b. Her father had changed.
    c. She wanted the old Eskimo life which her father could not offer her.
    d. All of the above

Julie of the Wolves Multiple Choice Study Guide/Quiz Questions Page 16

25. To what realization does Miyax come?
    a. She will be alone the rest of her life.
    b. The hour of the Eskimo and the wolf is over.
    c. The wolves are her only family now.
    d. Her father doesn't love her.

26. What are we made to believe at the end of the story?
    a. She returns to her father and adapts to the new life.
    b. She lives the rest of her life on the tundra.
    c. She goes to San Francisco.
    d. She returns to her home village.

ANSWER KEY: MULTIPLE CHOICE STUDY QUESTIONS
Julie of the Wolves

Part I		Part II	Part III	
1. A	20. A	1. B	1. A	14. B
2. A	21. A	2. A	2. B	15. C
3. C	22. B	3. A	3. C	16. D
4. B	23. A	4. D	4. D	17. B
5. A	24. C	5. C	5. C	18. A
6. C	25. B	6. B	6. A	19. C
7. D	26. C	7. A	7. B	20. D
8. A	27. D	8. B	8. B	21. B
9. B	28. D	9. D	9. D	22. C
10. C	29. A	10. C	10. D	23. D
11. A	30. C	11. B	11. C	24. D
12. B	31. B	12. D	12. A	25. B
13. D	32. B	13. A	13. B	26. A
14. C	33. A	14. C		
15. A	34. C	15. B		
16. C	35. B	16. A		
17. B	36. D	17. A		
18. C	37. A	18. C		
19. B		19. D		

PREREADING VOCABULARY WORKSHEETS

VOCABULARY - *Julie of the Wolves*

Part I: Using Prior Knowledge

Below are the sentences in which the vocabulary words appear in the text. Read the sentence. Use any clues you can find in the sentence combined with your prior knowledge, and write what you think the underlined words mean on the lines provided.

1. Her hands trembled and her heartbeat quickened for she was frightened...because of her desperate predicament.

   _____

2. She had been watching the wolves for two days, trying to discern which of their sounds and movements expressed goodwill and friendship.

   _____

3. She lay on the lichen-speckled frost heave in the midst of the bleak tundra.

   _____

4. Not a tree grew anywhere to break the monotony of the gold-green plain...

   _____

5. Each brick had been cut with her *ulo*, the half-moon shaped woman's knife, so versatile it can trim a baby's hair, slice a tough bear, or chip an iceberg.

   _____

6. Amaroq's tail flashed high as her mouthing charged him with vitality.

   _____

7. Intimidated, Jello pulled his ears together and back. He drew himself down until he looked smaller than ever.

   _____

8. Silver came up the long slope, gave the grunt whine that summoned the pups, and Kapu ran to meet her.

   _____

Julie of the Wolves Vocabulary Reading Assignment 1 Continued

9. When she had retrieved every <u>morsel</u> she gently closed her lips on the bridge of his nose.

_____

10. "More lichens grow on one side of the frost heaves than on the other." She <u>pondered</u> this...

_____

Part II. Matching

___ 1. Predicament   A. vigor, energy

___ 2. Discern   B. small piece or bite of food

___ 3. Tundra   C. considered carefully

___ 4. Monotony   D. called together

___ 5. Versatile   E. troublesome situation

___ 6. Vitality   F. having many uses

___ 7. Intimidated   G. to perceive something obscure or concealed

___ 8. Summoned   H. wearisome; sameness

___ 9. Morsel   I. discouraged and inhibited by or as if by threats

___ 10. Pondered   J. treeless area between ice cap and tree line in arctic regions

Vocabulary - *Julie of the Wolves* Reading Assignment #2

Part I: Using Contextual Clues

Below are the sentences in which the vocabulary words appear in the text. Read the sentence. Use any clues you can find in the sentence combined with your prior knowledge, and write what you think the underlined words mean on the lines provided.

11. "Change your ways when fear <u>seizes</u>," he had said, "for it usually means you are doing something wrong."

_____

12. His tail beat again and she scrambled to her house, <u>awed</u> by the sensitivity of Amaroq.

_____

13. When she tired of these melodies she <u>improvised</u> on the songs of her childhood.

_____

14. The engines <u>accelerated</u>, and the plane sped off in what must be the direction of Fairbanks.

_____

15. Nails barked. Then Amaroq slid into a musical <u>crescendo</u> that Silver joined in.

_____

16. With a <u>deft</u> twist of the ulo, she cut off a slice and savored each bite of this, the most nourishing part of the animal.

_____

17. Hearing anger in her voice he stood up, the hairs on his back rising <u>menacingly</u>.

_____

18. He was indeed a <u>lowly</u> wolf - a poor spirit, with fears and without friends.

_____

Julie of the Wolves Vocabulary Reading Assignment 2 Continued

Part II. Matching

___ 11. Seizes   A. increased in speed
___ 12. Awed   B. threateningly
___ 13. Improvised   C. gradual increase in volume
___ 14. Accelerated   D. skillful
___ 15. Crescendo   E. grabs hold of
___ 16. Deft   G. invented without preparation for rehearsal
___ 17. Menacingly   H. suited for a low rank; meek & humble
___ 18. Lowly   I. having an emotion of mixed reverence, dread and wonder

Vocabulary - *Julie of the Wolves* Reading Assignment #3

Part I: Using Contextual Clues

Below are the sentences in which the vocabulary words appear in the text. Read the sentence. Use any clues you can find in the sentence combined with your prior knowledge, and write what you think the underlined words mean on the lines provided.

19. The feathered horns of the comical puffins drooped low, and Kapugen told her they seemed to be grieving with him.

   _____

20. They would wade out into the river mouth where the stone weirs were built and drive the fish into nets between the walls.

   _____

21. "Your father," she said, "went seal hunting in that ridiculous kayak.

   _____

22. The pilot himself escorted her up the steps into the gleaming cabin.

   _____

23. Most of these arrangements are for convenience. I'm sure you are here to help Nusan make parkas and mittens for the tourists."

   _____

24. The top of the world began to glow like an eclipse as the sun circled just below the horizon.

   _____

25. "tomorrow, tomorrow, I can, I can, can, can, ha ha," he bleated piteously.

   _____

47

Julie of the Wolves Vocabulary Reading Assignment 3 Continued

Part II. Matching

___ 19. Grieving   A. pathetically
___ 20. Weirs   B. accompanied to give guidance or protection
___ 21. Ridiculous   C. the obscuring of one celestial body by another
___ 22. Escorted   D. fences put in a stream to catch fish or divert water
___ 23. Convenience   E. absurd; preposterous; laughable
___ 24. Eclipse   F. anything that makes work less difficult
___ 25. Piteously   G. mourning

Vocabulary *Julie of the Wolves* Reading Assignment #4

Part I: Using Contextual Clues

Below are the sentences in which the vocabulary words appear in the text. Read the sentence. Use any clues you can find in the sentence combined with your prior knowledge, and write what you think the underlined words mean on the lines provided.

26. Holding him in abeyance with the antler, she glanced around the ruins of her home and took stock of the damage.

_____

27. She dug a niche in the side of a heave with her man's knife.

_____

28. The first bark was one of inquiry, a sort of "Where are you and what are you doing?"

_____

29. The next call, however, was disquieting. The wolf seemed to be saying there was danger in the air.

_____

30. She cut the drag in two pieces and pushing the poles under one piece, she erected a tent.

_____

31. She stepped forward on the vast stage at the top of the world and bowed to her immense audience.

_____

32. When it continued to zag she realized the pilot was following a meandering river where game wintered.

_____

Julie of the Wolves Vocabulary Reading Assignment 4 Continued

Part II. Matching

___ 26. Abeyance   A. a steep, shallow recess in a rock or hill
___ 27. Niche   B. troubling
___ 28. Inquiry   C. huge
___ 29. Disquieting   D. the condition of being temporarily set aside
___ 30. Erected   E. following a winding course
___ 31. Immense   F. a question
___ 32. Meandering   G. set up

Vocabulary *Julie of the Wolves* Reading Assignment #5

Part I: Using Contextual Clues

Below are the sentences in which the vocabulary words appear in the text. Read the sentence. Use any clues you can find in the sentence combined with your prior knowledge, and write what you think the underlined words mean on the lines provided.

33. Miyax found the clear nights quite manageable.

___

34. They were forced to hunt rabbits and small game. These would not sustain them

___

35. Game would be more abundant in the dwarf willows and aspens that bordered the waterways.

___

36. The snow glowed blue and green and the constellations glittered, not only in the sky, but on the ice in the river and on the snow on the bushes and trees.

___

37. There, as she suspected, lay several rabbits and ptarmigan.

___

38. He had become enamored of hunting and fishing.

___

39. She hoisted her pack to her back and picked up Tornait.

___

40. Miyax has seen this game in Barrow, and she watched the flying figures with fascination.

___

Julie of the Wolves Vocabulary Reading Assignment 5 Continued

41. She was <u>engulfed</u> in light for an instant, then the door closed behind her.

_____

Part II. Matching

   ___ 33. Manageable   A. to surmise to be true or probable
   ___ 34. Sustain   B. irresistible attraction
   ___ 35. Abundant   C. raised up; lifted up
   ___ 36. Constellations   D. inspired with love; captivated; charmed
   ___ 37. Suspected   E. maintain; prolong; keep in existence
   ___ 38. Enamored   F. surrounded completely
   ___ 39. Hoisted   G. in plentiful supply
   ___ 40. Fascination   H. able to be handled or controlled
   ___ 41. Engulfed   I. formations of stars

ANSWER KEY: VOCABULARY
Julie of the Wolves

1. E	11. E	20. D	27. A	34. E
2. G	12. I	21. E	28. F	35. G
3. J	13. G	22. B	29. B	36. I
4. H	14. A	23. F	30. G	37. A
5. F	15. C	24. C	31. C	38. D
6. A	16. D	25. A	32. E	39. C
7. I	17. B	26. D	33. H	40. B
8. D	18. H			41. F
9. B	19. G			
10. C				

DAILY LESSONS

LESSON ONE

Objectives
1. To introduce the unit
2. To distribute books and other related materials
3. To give students some background information about Alaska and the Eskimos
3. To preview the study questions for chapters 1-3
4. To familiarize students with the vocabulary for chapters 1-3

Activity #1
Show students a film about Alaska and the Eskimos so they can have a clear idea of the climate and the ways of the Eskimos.

Activity #2
Distribute the materials students will use in this unit. Explain in detail how students are to use these materials.

Study Guides Students should read the study guide questions for each reading assignment prior to beginning the reading assignment to get a feeling for what events and ideas are important in the section they are about to read. After reading the section, students will (as a class or individually) answer the questions to review the important events and ideas from that section of the book. Students should keep the study guides as study materials for the unit test.

Vocabulary Prior to reading a reading assignment, students will do vocabulary work related to the section of the book they are about to read. Following the completion of the reading of the book, there will be a vocabulary review of all the words used in the vocabulary assignments. Students should keep their vocabulary work as study materials for the unit test.

Reading Assignment Sheet You need to fill in the reading assignment sheet to let students know by when their reading has to be completed. You can either write the assignment sheet up on a side blackboard or bulletin board and leave it there for students to see each day, or you can "ditto" copies for each student to have. In either case, you should advise students to become very familiar with the reading assignments so they know what is expected of them.

Extra Activities Center The Extra Activities portion of this unit contains suggestions for an extra library of related books and articles in your classroom as well as crossword and word search puzzles. Make an extra activities center in your room where you will keep these materials for students to use. (Bring the books and articles in from the library and keep several copies of the puzzles on hand.) Explain to students that these materials are available for students to use when they finish reading assignments or other class work early.

<u>Nonfiction Assignment Sheet</u> Explain to students that they each are to read at least one non-fiction piece related in some way to *Julie of the Wolves* at some time during the unit. Students will fill out a nonfiction assignment sheet after completing the reading to help you evaluate their reading experiences and to help the students think about and evaluate their own reading experiences.

<u>Books</u> Each school has its own rules and regulations regarding student use of school books. Advise students of the procedures that are normal for your school.

<u>Activity #3</u>
Preview the study questions and have students do the vocabulary work for Reading Assignment 1 of *Julie of the Wolves*. If students do not finish this assignment during this class period, they should complete it prior to the next class meeting.

NONFICTION ASSIGNMENT SHEET - *Julie of the Wolves*
(To be completed after reading the required nonfiction article)

Name _____ Date _____

Title of Nonfiction Read _____

Written By _____ Publication Date _____

I. Factual Summary: Write a short summary of the piece you read.

II. Vocabulary
   1. With which vocabulary words in the piece did you encounter some degree of difficulty?

   2. How did you resolve your lack of understanding with these words?

III. Interpretation: What was the main point the author wanted you to get from reading his work?

IV. Criticism
   1. With which points of the piece did you agree or find easy to accept? Why?

   2. With which points of the piece did you disagree or find difficult to believe? Why?

V. Personal Response: What do you think about this piece? OR How does this piece influence your ideas?

LESSON TWO

Objectives
1. To read Assignment 1
2. To give students practice reading orally
3. To evaluate students' oral reading
4. To preview the study questions and vocabulary for Assignment 2

Activity #1

Have students read Assignment 1 for *Julie of the Wolves* out loud in class. You probably know the best way to get readers with your class; pick students at random, ask for volunteers, or use whatever method works best for your group. If you have not yet completed an oral reading evaluation for your students this marking period, this would be a good opportunity to do so. A form is included with this unit for your convenience.

Activity #2

Tell students that prior to the next class period they should preview the study questions and do the prereading vocabulary work for Assignment 2. Also, if students do not complete the first reading assignment in class, they should do so prior to the next class period.

LESSON THREE

Objectives
1. To read Assignment 2
2. To continue the oral reading evaluations
3. To preview the study questions and vocabulary work for Assignment 3

Activity #1

Have students read Assignment 2 orally. Continue the oral reading evaluations.

Activity #2

Tell students that prior to the next class period they should preview the study questions and do the prereading vocabulary work for Assignment 3. Also, if students do not complete the second reading assignment in class, they should do so prior to the next class period.

ORAL READING EVALUATION - *Julie of the Wolves*

Name _____ Class____ Date _____

SKILL	EXCELLENT	GOOD	AVERAGE	FAIR	POOR
Fluency	5	4	3	2	1
Clarity	5	4	3	2	1
Audibility	5	4	3	2	1
Pronunciation	5	4	3	2	1
_____	5	4	3	2	1
_____	5	4	3	2	1

Total _____   Grade _____

Comments:

LESSON FOUR

Objectives
    1. To review the main events and ideas from Part I
    2. To read Assignment 3 (Part II)

Activity #1

Give students a few minutes to formulate answers for the study guide questions for Part I, and then discuss the answers to the questions in detail. Write the answers on the board or overhead transparency so students can have the correct answers for study purposes.

Note: It is a good practice in public speaking and leadership skills for individual students to take charge of leading the discussions of the study questions. Perhaps a different student could go to the front of the class and lead the discussion each day that the study questions are discussed during this unit. Of course, the teacher should guide the discussion when appropriate and be sure to fill in any gaps the students leave.

Activity #2

Assign students to read Assignment 3 for *Julie of the Wolves* prior to your next class period. If there is time remaining in this period, students may begin reading silently.

LESSON FIVE

Objectives
1. To check to see that students read Assignment 3 as assigned
2. To review the main ideas and events from Part II
3. To give students the opportunity to practice writing to inform
4. To review the facts and situation of Miyax's life
5. To practice writing in a letter format
6. To give the teacher the opportunity to evaluate students' writing skills
7. To help students identify with Miyax

Activity #1

Quiz - Distribute quizzes and give students about 10 minutes to complete them. (Note: The quizzes may either be the short answer study guides or the multiple choice version for Part II.) Have students exchange papers. Grade the quizzes as a class. Collect the papers for recording the grades. (If you used the multiple choice version as a quiz, take a few minutes to discuss the answers for the short answer version if your students are using the short answer version for their study guides.)

Activity #2

Distribute Writing Assignment #1 and discuss the directions in detail. Give students ample time to complete the assignment and then collect the papers for grading.

NOTE: If your students need help with the letter format, place a sample letter on the board or overhead projector and discuss the basic elements of a friendly letter.

Activity #3

Tell students that prior to Lesson Six (give students a day and a date) they should preview the study questions and do the prereading vocabulary work for Assignment 4.

WRITING ASSIGNMENT #1 - *Julie of the Wolves*

PROMPT

In the first lesson of this unit you were introduced to some basic facts about the Eskimos and their way of life. Through reading the first two parts of *Julie of the Wolves*, you have seen first-hand the life of one Eskimo girl.

Your assignment is to write Miyax's first pen pal letter to Amy in which she describes her life to Amy, who is from San Francisco.

PREWRITING

One way to begin is to jot down everything you can remember (or can find by skimming your book and/or notes) about Miyax's life. You may supplement the facts of the story with facts you learned in the first lesson of this unit.

Now, pretend you are Miyax. Organize these facts about your life into some logical order so that they will make sense to Amy. You might start with some background information about your life, give a short account of your daily activities, and then discuss your current situation in life and your hopes for the future.

DRAFTING

Open your letter in a letter format. Introduce yourself in the first paragraph, perhaps explaining how you have become Amy's new pen pal.

Spend a paragraph discussing your personal background. Take another paragraph to inform Amy about your daily activities. Make another paragraph telling Amy about your current situation in life--things that are going on in your life and how you feel about them.

Close your letter with a paragraph telling Amy about your hopes for the future.

Perhaps include a P.S. asking a question or two for Amy to answer in her next letter.

PROMPT

When you finish the rough draft of your paper, ask a student who sits near you to read it. After reading your rough draft, he/she should tell you what he/she liked best about your work, which parts were difficult to understand, and ways in which your work could be improved. Reread your paper considering your critic's comments, and make the corrections you think are necessary.

PROOFREADING

Do a final proofreading of your paper double-checking your grammar, spelling, organization, and the clarity of your ideas.

LESSON SIX

Objectives

    1. To read Assignment 4

    2. To preview the study questions and do the prereading vocabulary work for Assignment 5

    3. To read Assignment 5

Activity

    Tell students that prior to Lesson Eight (give students a day and a date), they should have read Assignment 4, have done the previewing and prereading work for Assignment 5, and have read Assignment 5. Give students this class period to work on these assignments.

LESSON SEVEN

Objectives

    1. To prepare students for the group activity & writing assignment which will follow

    2. To give students a break from the ordinary read-question-answer routine

    3. To instruct students in basic camping and survival skills

Activity

    Invite a local Boy Scout (or Girl Scout or Outward Bound) leader to come in to your classroom and discuss camping and survival techniques. He (or she) should be sure to include information about basic equipment and skills, some "tricks of the trade" students might find useful on a camping trip, and pointers as to how to plan a camping trip.

    Spend this class period listening to the guest's presentation and giving students ample time to ask questions of their own.

LESSON EIGHT

Objectives
    1. To review the main events of Part III
    2. To review all of the vocabulary work done in this unit

Activity #1
    Give students a quiz on Part III. Use either the short answer or multiple choice form of the study guide questions as a quiz so that in discussing the answers to the quiz you also answer the study guide questions. Collect the papers for grade recording.

Activity #2
    Choose one (or more) of the vocabulary review activities listed on the next page(s) and spend your class period as directed in the activity. Some of the materials for these review activities are located in the Vocabulary Resource section of this unit. If your students need more work with the vocabulary words, use some of the extra vocabulary materials provided in this unit for homework, extra class work, or extra credit work.

VOCABULARY REVIEW ACTIVITIES

1. Divide your class into two teams and have an old-fashioned spelling or definition bee.

2. Give each of your students (or students in groups of two, three or four) a *Julie of the Wolves* Vocabulary Word Search Puzzle. The person (group) to find all of the vocabulary words in the puzzle first wins.

3. Give students a *Julie of the Wolves* Vocabulary Word Search Puzzle without the word list. The person or group to find the most vocabulary words in the puzzle wins.

4. Use a *Julie of the Wolves* Vocabulary Crossword Puzzle. Put the puzzle onto a transparency on the overhead projector (so everyone can see it), and do the puzzle together as a class.

5. Give students a *Julie of the Wolves* Vocabulary Matching Worksheet to do.

6. Divide your class into two teams. Use the *Julie of the Wolves* vocabulary words with their letters jumbled as a word list. Student 1 from Team A faces off against Student 1 from Team B. You write the first jumbled word on the board. The first student (1A or 1B) to unscramble the word wins the chance for his/her team to score points. If 1A wins the jumble, go to student 2A and give him/her a definition. He/she must give you the correct spelling of the vocabulary word which fits that definition. If he/she does, Team A scores a point, and you give student 3A a definition for which you expect a correctly spelled matching vocabulary word. Continue giving Team A definitions until some team member makes an incorrect response. An incorrect response sends the game back to the jumbled-word face off, this time with students 2A and 2B. Instead of repeating giving definitions to the first few students of each team, continue with the student after the one who gave the last incorrect response on the team. For example, if Team B wins the jumbled-word face-off, and student 5B gave the last incorrect answer for Team B, you would start this round of definition questions with student 6B, and so on. The team with the most points wins!

7. Have students write a story in which they correctly use as many vocabulary words as possible. Have students read their compositions orally! Post the most original compositions on your bulletin board!

LESSON NINE

Objective

To discuss *Julie of the Wolves* on a deeper than direct-recall level beyond the basic facts of the story

Activity #1

Choose the questions from the Extra Discussion Questions/Writing Assignments which seem most appropriate for your students. A class discussion of these questions is most effective if students have been given the opportunity to formulate answers to the questions prior to the discussion. To this end, you may either have all the students formulate answers to all the questions, divide your class into groups and assign one or more questions to each group, or you could assign one question to each student in your class. The option you choose will make a difference in the amount of class time needed for this activity.

Activity #3

After students have had ample time to formulate answers to the questions, begin your class discussion of the questions and the ideas presented by the questions. Be sure students take notes during the discussion so they have information to study for the unit test.

LESSON TEN

Objectives

1. To give students feedback about their first writing assignments
2. To help students with the revising and editing of their first writing assignments
3. To give students the opportunity to practice writing to persuade
4. To give the teacher the opportunity to evaluate students' writing skills
5. To have students role play to look at Julie's life from Amy's point of view after she has received Julie's introductory letter (writing assignment #1).

Activity #1

Distribute Writing Assignment #2 and discuss the directions in detail. Give your students ample time to complete the assignment and then collect the papers for grading.

Activity #2

While students begin working on Writing Assignment #2, call students to your desk (or some other private area) to discuss their papers from Writing Assignment 1. A Writing Evaluation Form is included with this unit to help structure your conferences.

Students should try to apply the suggestions you make about their first writing assignments to their second assignments. Also have students go ahead and make the corrections you suggest in their first writing assignments and have them hand the first assignments back in to you (give students a day and a date that they will be due) for another grading.

EXTRA WRITING ASSIGNMENTS/DISCUSSION QUESTIONS - *Julie of the Wolves*

Interpretation

1. Identify each of the wolves in the pack by name and give each one's major characteristics.

2. When and why was Miyax called "Julie"?

3. What is the importance of the setting?

4. What are the conflicts in the story? Are they resolved? If so, how? If not, why not?

5. From what point of view is the story written? How does that affect our attitudes as we read?

6. Describe at least five of the clever ways Miyax survived in the wilderness.

7. Where is the climax of the story? Explain your choice.

8. What are the major coincidences in the book? Of what use are they?

Critical

9 Explain how Miyax changes during the course of the story.

10. What is Mr. Pollock's role in the story?

11. What function does each of the following characters serve in the novel: Aunt Martha, Amy, Daniel, Judith, Naka, and Tornait?

12. Why did Julie point her boots towards Kapugen?

13. Explain the significance or importance of each of the following in the story: ulo, totem, oil drum, skua, gussak, bladders, North Star, and airplane.

14. What does "adapt" mean? Give all the examples of it you can find in this book.

15. Discuss the treatment of "gussaks" in the book. Are they shown as being good or bad?

16. Compare and contrast "wolf civilization" with man's civilization.

Julie of the Wolves Extra Discussion Questions Page 2

Critical/Personal Response

17. Is the story of *Julie of the Wolves* believable? Explain why or why not.

18. Discuss the idea of survival of the fittest as it relates to the novel.

19. What messages are presented to the reader of this book?

20. Why was Miyax able to survive in the wilderness? What did she have in her favor?

21. Was Kapugen right to arrange Miyax's marriage, leave and not come back again? Why or why not?

Personal Response

22. Miyax's life changed considerably during the course of the novel. Sometimes things happen in our lives and we just have to deal with the change, pick up and move on with life. What are some of those kinds of events that affect our lives?

23. How does civilization compare to life in the wild in this story?

24. The Eskimos are not the only group of people to lose some of their cultural heritage in the great melting pot of America. What are some other groups of people who have also lost some of their traditions?

25. If it were your decision, what choice would you have made at the end of the story? Would you have made the same decision that Miyax did? Why or why not?

26. Which part of the story did you enjoy most? Which was your least favorite?

27. Have you seen any movies or read any other books about people who get lost in a wilderness? What were they? How did they compare to *Julie of the Wolves*?

WRITING ASSIGNMENT #2 - *Julie of the Wolves*

PROMPT

You have written a letter of introduction to Amy. Now you are to pretend you are Amy. You have received Julie's first letter and have been corresponding with her. Now you are to write a letter to Julie persuading her to come to San Francisco to live with your family.

PREWRITING

You are Amy. Make a list of the good things about Julie's life in Alaska. Make a list of the bad points of Julie's life in Alaska. Make a list of reasons you <u>want</u> Julie to come live with you. Make a list of reasons why Julie might want to come live with you.

Now look at your lists. The purpose of your letter is to persuade Julie to come live with you in San Francisco. What item in all of your lists would be the most likely to persuade Julie to come live with you? (Consider this from Julie's point of view.) Put a star next to that item. What three other reasons do you think would most likely convince Julie to come live with you? Number these reasons 1, 2, and 3 from most likely to least likely.

DRAFTING

One way to begin is to write a paragraph in which you introduce the idea that you would like Julie to come live with you and your family in San Francisco. You may use any approach you think would be appropriate to bring up this topic.

Begin the body of your paper with a paragraph about the item you have put a star next to on your list. Continue the body of your paragraph with a paragraph for each of the other three main reasons you think Julie should come live with you.

Write a concluding paragraph in which you try to stress your points one last time, make a final pitch or plea and then let Julie know that you'll be waiting to hear from her.

Close and sign your letter.

NOTE: There are many different ways this letter could be written. This is just one way. Stop and think for yourself: If you were writing to Julie, how would you persuade her to come stay with your family? The object of this assignment is for you to persuade Julie to come live with you; feel free to use whatever means you think will be most effective.

PROOFREADING

When you finish the rough draft of your paper, ask a student who sits near you to read it. After reading your rough draft, he/she should tell you what he/she liked best about your work, which parts were difficult to understand, and ways in which your work could be improved. Reread your paper considering your critic's comments, and make the corrections you think are necessary.

Do a final proofreading of your paper double-checking your grammar, spelling, organization, and the clarity of your ideas.

WRITING EVALUATION FORM - *Julie of the Wolves*

Name _____ Date _____

Writing Assignment #1 for the *Julie of the Wolves* unit Grade _____

Circle One For Each Item:

Letter Format:	excellent	good	fair	poor
Character Analysis:	excellent	good	fair	poor
Grammar:	excellent	good	fair	poor
Spelling:	excellent	good	fair	poor
Punctuation:	excellent	good	fair	poor
Legibility:	excellent	good	fair	poor

Strengths:

Weaknesses:

Comments/Suggestions:

LESSONS ELEVEN AND TWELVE

Objectives
1. To have students actually plan a camping trip
2. To have students practice their skills of organizing and thinking logically

Activity

Divide your class into small groups of four to five students each. Explain that each group is to plan a camping trip, complete with all the details. A worksheet is provided to help students make their plans.

Give students these two class periods to work on their plans.

NOTES: Visit your local AAA club or travel bureau to get maps and information about places to camp and things to do near the campsites chosen. This will help students make their trips more interesting and more accurate.

To add interest to the unit, you could assign dollar values to students' participation in class, grades on assignments, attendance in class, etc. throughout the unit. The amount of money students accumulate in lessons one through twelve would then be the budget they would have to use on their camping trip. (Group members may pool all of their funds if they wish.) That would help to make the trip more realistic and would help students learn to budget.

LESSON THIRTEEN

Objectives
1. To fully complete the imaginary camping trip
2. To give students the opportunity to do some creative thinking and creative writing
3. To have students practice relating events in writing
4. To give the teacher the opportunity to evaluate students' writing skills
5. To give students the opportunity to write to express their own ideas and opinions

Activity #1

Distribute Writing Assignment #3. Discuss the directions in detail and give students ample time to complete the assignment. Collect the papers for grading.

NOTE: If your class was actually able to go on a camping trip, use Writing Assignment #3 for students to write about their actual trip.

Activity #2

Remind students that their nonfiction reports will be due in the next class period.

WORKSHEET - Camping Trip

Who is going?

How much money do you have to spend on this trip?

    Make a budget showing how much you will need to spend and for what.

When are you going?

    How long will you be gone? (minimum of 3 days and 2 nights required)

Where are you going?

    Will you stay in one place or travel during your trip?

What could the weather be like?

What equipment will you need?

    Who will bring the equipment, and where will they get it?

What personal gear will each person need to bring (clothing, toiletries, etc.)

How will you get to where you are going?

What provisions should you make for eating and drinking?

What will you do during each day of your trip?

What kinds of emergencies could occur, and how will you be equipped to deal with them?

Are there any special requirements that need to be considered for your trip?

Do you need anything from anyone other than yourselves? What arrangements must be made with the other people involved?

    What will you do if those other people do not do what they say they will do?

Is there anything else you can think of that you may have overlooked?

WRITING ASSIGNMENT #3 - *Julie of the Wolves*

PROMPT

You and some of your class mates have just planned a camping trip. Now you are to let your imagination loose and tell exactly what happened on your camping trip.

PREWRITING

Down the left-hand side of a sheet of paper write "Day 1," skip a few lines and write "Day 2," skip a few lines and write "Day 3," etc. for as many days as your camping trip lasted.

Next to (and under if necessary) each "Day" heading, jot down a few notes about what happened on that day of your trip. Refer to your camping trip worksheet and the materials you generated from that to refresh your memory as to where you were supposed to be each day. Where were you? How did you get there? Did anything interesting or unusual happen to you while you were there?

Be creative; consider the personalities of the people who went on the trip with you. What kinds of things could have happened? Include these kinds of things in your descriptions.

Think about your trip after you have filled in all of your "Days." What word(s) or phrase(s) would best describe your trip? Fun? Humiliating? Disastrous? Educational? Full of adventure?

DRAFTING

One way to begin is to write an introductory paragraph in which you introduce your reader to the idea that you took a trip.

The body of your composition could consist of one paragraph for each day of your trip. You may follow the rough outline that you jotted down while prewriting.

You should include a concluding paragraph in which you sum up your feelings and attitudes about your trip.

PROMPT

When you finish the rough draft of your paper, ask a student who sits near you to read it. After reading your rough draft, he/she should tell you what he/she liked best about your work, which parts were difficult to understand, and ways in which your work could be improved. Reread your paper considering your critic's comments, and make the corrections you think are necessary.

PROOFREADING

Do a final proofreading of your paper double-checking your grammar, spelling, organization, and the clarity of your ideas.

LESSON FOURTEEN

Objectives
    1. To widen the breadth of students' knowledge about the topics discussed or touched upon in *Julie of the Wolves*
    2. To check students' nonfiction reading assignments

Activity

    Ask each student to give a brief oral report about the nonfiction work he/she read for the nonfiction reading assignment. Your criteria for evaluating this report will vary depending on the level of your students. You may wish for students to give a complete report without using notes of any kind, or you may want students to read directly from a written report, or you may want to do something inbetween these two extremes. Just make students aware of your criteria in ample time for them to prepare their reports.

    Start with one student's report. After that, ask if anyone else in the class has read about a topic related to the first student's report. If no one has, choose another student at random. After each report, be sure to ask if anyone has a report related to the one just completed. That will help keep a continuity during the discussion of the reports.

LESSON FIFTEEN

Objective
    To review the main ideas presented in *Julie of the Wolves*

Activity #1

    Choose one of the review games/activities included in this unit and spend your class period as outlined there. Some materials for these activities are located in the Extra Activities section of this unit.

Activity #2

    Remind students that the Unit Test will be in the next class meeting. Stress the review of the Study Guides and their class notes as a last minute, brush-up review for homework.

REVIEW GAMES/ACTIVITIES - *Julie of the Wolves*

1. Ask the class to make up a unit test for *Julie of the Wolves*. The test should have 4 sections: matching, true/false, short answer, and essay. Students may use 1/2 period to make the test and then swap papers and use the other 1/2 class period to take a test a classmate has devised. (open book) You may want to use the unit test included in this unit or take questions from the students' unit tests to formulate your own test.

2. Take 1/2 period for students to make up true and false questions (including the answers). Collect the papers and divide the class into two teams. Draw a big tic-tac-toe board on the chalk board. Make one team X and one team O. Ask questions to each side, giving each student one turn. If the question is answered correctly, that students' team's letter (X or O) is placed in the box. If the answer is incorrect, no mark is placed in the box. The object is to get three marks in a row like tic-tac-toe. You may want to keep track of the number of games won for each team.

3. Take 1/2 period for students to make up questions (true/false and short answer). Collect the questions. Divide the class into two teams. You'll alternate asking questions to individual members of teams A & B (like in a spelling bee). The question keeps going from A to B until it is correctly answered, then a new question is asked. A correct answer does not allow the team to get another question. Correct answers are +2 points; incorrect answers are -1 point.

4. Have students pair up and quiz each other from their study guides and class notes.

5. Give students a *Julie of the Wolves* crossword puzzle to complete.

6. Divide your class into two teams. Use the *Julie of the Wolves* crossword words with their letters jumbled as a word list. Student 1 from Team A faces off against Student 1 from Team B. You write the first jumbled word on the board. The first student (1A or 1B) to unscramble the word wins the chance for his/her team to score points. If 1A wins the jumble, go to student 2A and give him/her a clue. He/she must give you the correct word which matches that clue. If he/she does, Team A scores a point, and you give student 3A a clue for which you expect another correct response. Continue giving Team A clues until some team member makes an incorrect response. An incorrect response sends the game back to the jumbled-word face off, this time with students 2A and 2B. Instead of repeating giving clues to the first few students of each team, continue with the student after the one who gave the last incorrect response on the team. For example, if Team B wins the jumbled-word face-off, and student 5B gave the last incorrect answer for Team B, you would start this round of clue questions with student 6B, and so on. The team with the most points wins!

UNIT TESTS

SHORT ANSWER UNIT TEST #1 - *Julie of the Wolves*

I. Matching/Identify

___ 1. Amaroq   A. Author

___ 2. Julie   B. Kapugen's serious partner

___ 3. George   C. Knife

___ 4. Amy   D. Coward; Amaroq killed him

___ 5. Ulo   E. Kapugen's new home village

___ 6. Kapugen   F. Leader of the pack

___ 7. Naka   G. New leader of the pack

___ 8. Jello   H. Pen pal

___ 9. Tornait   I. Non-Eskimo Americans

___ 10. Kapu   J. Hunter trained by Kapugen

___ 11. Kangik   K. Miyax

___ 12. Martha   L. Miyax's husband

___ 13. Gussaks   M. Plover

___ 14. Atik   N. Miyax's father

___ 15. Daniel   O. Miyax's aunt

Julie Short Answer Unit Test 1 Page 2

II. Short Answer

1. Why did Miyax choose the black wolf to help her?

2. What did Miyax want to do at Point Hope?

3. Why did the hunters return the bladders to the seals?

4. How could Miyax get away from Aunt Martha if she wanted to?

5. What did Miyax think of Daniel upon meeting him?

6. What was Kapugen's saying about fear?

7. What was Pearl to tell Nusan? Why?

Julie Short Answer Unit Test 1 Page 3

8. Where was Miyax going?

9. What are bounties and what did they encourage?

10. What did the oil drum mark?

11. What happened to Amaroq?

12. Why did Miyax move her pack to the river?

13. Who were Miyax's visitors?

14. Who did Miyax find in Kangik, and what did she discover about his lifestyle?

15. Why did Miyax leave her father?

16. To what realization does Miyax come?

17. What are we made to believe at the end of the story?

Julie Short Answer Unit Test 1 Page 4

III. Composition
    Write a letter from Julie to Amy in which she explains why she is not coming to San Francisco.

Julie Short Answer Unit Test 1 Page 5

IV. Vocabulary

Listen to the vocabulary words and spell them. After you have spelled all the words, go back and write down the definitions.

1.

2.

3.

4.

5.

6.

7.

8.

9.

10.

KEY: SHORT ANSWER UNIT TEST #1 - *Julie of the Wolves*

I. Matching

F	1. Amaroq	A. Author
K	2. Julie	B. Kapugen's serious partner
A	3. George	C. Knife
H	4. Amy	D. Coward; Amaroq killed him
C	5. Ulo	E. Kapugen's new home village
N	6. Kapugen	F. Leader of the pack
B	7. Naka	G. New leader of the pack
D	8. Jello	H. Pen pal
M	9. Tornait	I. Non-Eskimo Americans
G	10. Kapu	J. Hunter trained by Kapugen
E	11. Kangik	K. Miyax
O	12. Martha	L. Miyax's husband
I	13. Gussaks	M. Plover
J	14. Atik	N. Miyax's father
L	15. Daniel	O. Miyax's aunt

II. Short Answer

1. Why did Miyax choose the black wolf to help her?
    She chose him because he appeared to have wisdom and to be the leader.
2. What did Miyax want to do at Point Hope?
    She wanted to meet the ship, the North Star, and earn her way to San Francisco where her pen pal, Amy, lived.
3. Why did the hunters return the bladders to the seals?
    They believed that the bladders held the spirits of the seals. They returned the bladders so the spirits could enter the bodies of the newborn seals and keep them safe until harvest time.
4. How could Miyax get away from Aunt Martha if she wanted to?
    If she doesn't like living with Aunt Martha, Miyax may marry Daniel, Naka's son, when she is thirteen.
5. What did Miyax think of Daniel upon meeting him?
    She was disappointed because there was something wrong with him.
6. What was Kapugen's saying about fear?
    He said that when fear seizes, you should change what you are doing because you are doing something wrong.
7. What was Pearl to tell Nusan? Why?
    She was to tell Nusan that she saw Julie going out on the ice so Nusan would think Julie drowned and wouldn't look for her very long.
8. Where was Miyax going?
    She was going to San Francisco to see her pen pal, Amy Pollock.

9. What are bounties and what did they encourage?

    A bounty is a sum of money offered to anyone who brings in a certain kind of animal. Bounties encouraged killing for money instead of for need.

10. What did the oil drum mark?

    It marked the beginning of civilization.

11. What happened to Amaroq?

    The hunters in the plane shot and killed him and never even came back for his body.

12. Why did Miyax move her pack to the river?

    There were more animals for them to find to eat at the river.

13. Who were Miyax's visitors?

    A hunter and his wife and child happened upon Miyax's home.

14. Who did Miyax find in Kangik, and what did she discover about his lifestyle?

    She found Kapugen, her father. At first she was pleased because his house looked just like their house at the hunting camp, but when she discovered that he had a wife and that he had adopted many of the modern ways of man, she was disappointed.

15. Why did Miyax leave her father?

    The father she remembered was dead to her; he had changed. She wanted the old life, which he could no longer offer her.

16. To what realization does Miyax come?

    She realizes that "the hour of the wolf and the Eskimo is over."

17. What are we made to believe at the end of the story?

    Julie returns to her father and learns to adapt to the more modern culture, accepting that the old ways are pretty much gone.

III. Composition: Answers will vary.

IV. Vocabulary

   Choose ten of the vocabulary words to read orally to your class for Part IV of the Unit test.

SHORT ANSWER UNIT TEST #2 - *Julie of the Wolves*

___ 1. Amaroq   A. Kapugen's new home village

___ 2. Julie   B. Pen pal

___ 3. George   C. Miyax

___ 4. Amy   D. Leader of the pack

___ 5. Ulo   E. Author

___ 6. Kapugen   F. Non-Eskimo Americans

___ 7. Naka   G. Miyax's husband

___ 8. Jello   H. Kapugen's serious partner

___ 9. Tornait   I. Coward; Amaroq killed him

___ 10. Kapu   J. Hunter trained by Kapugen

___ 11. Kangik   K. Knife

___ 12. Martha   L. Miyax's aunt

___ 13. Gussaks   M. Plover

___ 14. Atik   N. Miyax's father

___ 15. Daniel   O. New leader of the pack

Julie Short Answer Unit Test 2 Page 2

II. Short Answer

1. What happened to Miyax's father?

2. Why did Miyax speak half in English and half Eskimo when she said, "Amaroq, Daya, wolf, my friend"?

3. What did Miyax want to do at Point Hope?

4. Why did the hunters return the bladders to the seals?

5. How could Miyax get away from Aunt Martha if she wanted to?

6. What was Kapugen's saying about fear?

7. What was Pearl to tell Nusan? Why?

8. How did Jello die?

Julie Short Answer Unit Test 2 Page 3

9. What are bounties and what did they encourage?

10. What happened to Amaroq?

11. Why did Miyax move her pack to the river?

12. Who did Miyax find in Kangik, and what did she discover about his lifestyle?

13. Why did Miyax leave her father?

14. What are we made to believe at the end of the story?

Julie Short Answer Unit Test 2 Page 4

III. Composition

Near the end of the story Miyax realizes that "the hour of the wolf and the Eskimo is over." What does that mean, and what things have led Miyax to that realization?

Julie Short Answer Unit Test 2 Page 5

IV. Vocabulary

Listen to the vocabulary words and spell them. After you have spelled all the words, go back and write down the definitions.

1.

2.

3.

4.

5.

6.

7.

8.

9.

10.

KEY: SHORT ANSWER UNIT TEST #2 - *Julie of the Wolves*

D	1. Amaroq	A.	Kapugen's new home village
C	2. Julie	B.	Pen pal
E	3. George	C.	Miyax
B	4. Amy	D.	Leader of the pack
K	5. Ulo	E.	Author
N	6. Kapugen	F.	Non-Eskimo Americans
H	7. Naka	G.	Miyax's husband
I	8. Jello	H.	Kapugen's serious partner
M	9. Tornait	I.	Coward; Amaroq killed him
O	10. Kapu	J.	Hunter trained by Kapugen
A	11. Kangik	K.	Knife
L	12. Martha	L.	Miyax's aunt
F	13. Gussaks	M.	Plover
J	14. Atik	N.	Miyax's father
G	15. Daniel	O.	New leader of the pack

II. Short Answer

1. What happened to Miyax's father?

    He paddled his kayak into the Bering Sea and disappeared.

2. Why did Miyax speak half in English and half Eskimo when she said, "Amaroq, Daya, wolf, my friend"?

    She hoped the wolf would understand her sentiments in one of the languages she knew.

3. What did Miyax want to do at Point Hope?

    She wanted to meet the ship, the North Star, and earn her way to San Francisco where her pen pal, Amy, lived.

4. Why did the hunters return the bladders to the seals?

    They believed that the bladders held the spirits of the seals. They returned the bladders so the spirits could enter the bodies of the newborn seals and keep them safe until harvest time.

5. How could Miyax get away from Aunt Martha if she wanted to?

    If she doesn't like living with Aunt Martha, Miyax may marry Daniel, Naka's son, when she is thirteen.

6. What was Kapugen's saying about fear?

    He said that when fear seizes, you should change what you are doing because you are doing something wrong.

7. What was Pearl to tell Nusan? Why?

    She was to tell Nusan that she saw Julie going out on the ice so Nusan would think Julie drowned and wouldn't look for her very long.

8. How did Jello die?

    Amaroq fought with him and killed him because he had done something bad to Miyax.

9. What are bounties and what did they encourage?
　　A bounty is a sum of money offered to anyone who brings in a certain kind of animal. Bounties encouraged killing for money instead of for need.
10. What happened to Amaroq?
　　The hunters in the plane shot and killed him and never even came back for his body.
11. Why did Miyax move her pack to the river?
　　There were more animals for them to find to eat at the river.
12. Who did Miyax find in Kangik, and what did she discover about his lifestyle?
　　She found Kapugen, her father. At first she was pleased because his house looked just like their house at the hunting camp, but when she discovered that he had a wife and that he had adopted many of the modern ways of man, she was disappointed.
13. Why did Miyax leave her father?
　　The father she remembered was dead to her; he had changed. She wanted the old life, which he could no longer offer her.
14. What are we made to believe at the end of the story?
　　Julie returns to her father and learns to adapt to the more modern culture, accepting that the old ways are pretty much gone.

III. Composition: Answers will vary.

IV. Vocabulary
　　Choose ten of the vocabulary words from this unit. Read them orally to your class for Part IV of the unit test.

ADVANCED SHORT ANSWER UNIT TEST - *Julie of the Wolves*

___ 1. Amaroq   A. Kapugen's new home village

___ 2. Julie   B. Pen pal

___ 3. George   C. Miyax

___ 4. Amy   D. Leader of the pack

___ 5. Ulo   E. Author

___ 6. Kapugen   F. Non-Eskimo Americans

___ 7. Naka   G. Miyax's husband

___ 8. Jello   H. Kapugen's serious partner

___ 9. Tornait   I. Coward; Amaroq killed him

___ 10. Kapu   J. Hunter trained by Kapugen

___ 11. Kangik   K. Knife

___ 12. Martha   L. Miyax's aunt

___ 13. Gussaks   M. Plover

___ 14. Atik   N. Miyax's father

___ 15. Daniel   O. New leader of the pack

Julie Advanced Short Answer Unit Test Page 2

II. Short Answer

1. Explain how Miyax changes during the course of the novel.

2. When and why is Miyax called "Julie"?

3. What major coincidences occur in the book? Of what use are they?

4. What function does each of the following characters serve in the novel: Aunt Martha, Amy, Daniel, Judith, Naka, and Tornait?

5. Identify each of the wolves in the pack by name and give each one's major characteristics.

Julie Advanced Short Answer Unit Test Page 3

6. Describe at least five of the clever ways Miyax survived in the wilderness.

7. What does "adapt" mean? Give all the examples of it that you can think of from the book.

8. Discuss the treatment of "gussaks" in the book. Are they shown as being good or bad? How and why?

9. In what ways does Miyax exemplify the traditional riches of Eskimo life: intelligence, fearlessness and love?

Julie Advanced Short Answer Unit Test Page 4

IV. Vocabulary

Listen to the vocabulary words and write them down. Later go back and write a short composition relating to *Julie of the Wolves* using all of these vocabulary words.

MULTIPLE CHOICE UNIT TEST 1 - *Julie of the Wolves*

I. Matching

___ 1. Amaroq   A. Author

___ 2. Julie   B. Kapugen's serious partner

___ 3. George   C. Knife

___ 4. Amy   D. Coward; Amaroq killed him

___ 5. Ulo   E. Kapugen's new home village

___ 6. Kapugen   F. Leader of the pack

___ 7. Naka   G. New leader of the pack

___ 8. Jello   H. Pen pal

___ 9. Tornait   I. Non-Eskimo Americans

___ 10. Kapu   J. Hunter trained by Kapugen

___ 11. Kangik   K. Miyax

___ 12. Martha   L. Miyax's husband

___ 13. Gussaks   M. Plover

___ 14. Atik   N. Miyax's father

___ 15. Daniel   O. Miyax's aunt

Julie Multiple Choice Unit Test 1 Page 2

II. Multiple Choice

1. What happened to Miyax's father?
   a. He got lost on a hunting trip.
   b. He paddled his kayak into the Bering Sea and disappeared.
   c. He died of old age.
   d. He had a sledding accident.

2. How did the author describe Miyax?
   a. "Tomboy-ish"
   b. "Pretty but rugged"
   c. "Healthy and natural"
   d. "Classic Eskimo beauty"

3. Why did Miyax speak half in English and half Eskimo when she said, "Amaroq, Daya, wolf, my friend"?
   a. She was hoping he would understand some part of the two languages she knew.
   b. Since she was going to San Francisco, she wanted to practice English.
   c. She naturally spoke both languages.
   d. She was delirious.

4. To where did Miyax intend to walk?
   a. San Francisco
   b. Point Hope
   c. Nunivak Island
   d. Barrow, Alaska

5. How did Miyax know the direction to Fairbanks?
   a. She saw the skyline of the city on the horizon.
   b. She calculated the direction based on the location of the North Star.
   c. She saw a plane flying over and assumed it was going to Fairbanks.
   d. She used her maps.

6. Why did the hunters return the bladders to the seals?
   a. So they could be used again
   b. No particular reason; they just did
   c. So the spirits could enter the bodies of the newborn seals
   d. So they wouldn't be wasted

Julie Multiple Choice Unit Test 1 Page 3

7. How did Miyax react when Kapugen called her Julie?
	a. She didn't care.
	b. She winked at him.
	c. She preferred to be called Julie.
	d. She got angry.

8. How could Miyax get away from Aunt Martha if she wanted to?
	a. She could marry Daniel.
	b. She could spend her vacations with her father.
	c. She could board at school.
	d. She could go work for Nusan.

9. What did Miyax think of Daniel upon meeting him?
	a. She thought he was a slob.
	b. She fell instantly in love with him.
	c. She liked him well enough and though he'd make a good husband.
	d. She was disappointed.

10. What was Kapugen's saying about fear?
	a. Rational thought conquers fear.
	b. If you are afraid, close your eyes and think a happy thought.
	c. When fear seizes, change what you are doing because you are doing something wrong.
	d. Fear is an enemy only in your mind.

11. What was Pearl to tell Nusan?
	a. She saw Julie headed back to Aunt Martha's house.
	b. She saw Julie going out on the ice.
	c. She saw Julie headed towards Judith's house.
	d. She saw Julie trying to kill herself.

12. How did Jello die?
	a. Hunters killed him.
	b. Amaroq killed him.
	c. Miyax killed him.
	d. Kapugen killed him.

Julie Multiple Choice Unit Test 1 Page 4

13. What did the fact that she saw a skua tell Miyax?
   a. She was getting closer to the ocean.
   b. Other people had recently been there.
   c. Spring had come.
   d. Caribou were near.

14. What did bounties encourage?
   a. Fighting among the Eskimos
   b. Farmers
   c. Killing for money instead of need
   d. Settlers

15. What happened to Amaroq?
   a. He drowned after falling through thin ice.
   b. Kapu killed him.
   c. He starved to death.
   d. Hunters killed him.

16. What problem did Amaroq's death cause for the wolf pack?
   a. They were all going their separate ways.
   b. They were fighting among themselves and killed each other off.
   c. They were starving without a leader.
   d. They weren't sleeping and were becoming vicious.

17. Why did Miyax move her pack to the river?
   a. There were more animals to kill for food at the river.
   b. There were no hunters at the river.
   c. The pack needed fresh water.
   d. Miyax wanted to follow the river to Point Hope.

18. Why did Miyax leave her father?
   a. Her wolves posed a danger to her father's village.
   b. She wanted to go to San Francisco.
   c. She wanted the old Eskimo life which her father could not offer her.
   d. All of the above

Julie Multiple Choice Unit Test 1 Page 5

19. To what realization does Miyax come?
    a. She will be alone the rest of her life.
    b. Her father doesn't love her.
    c. The wolves are her only family now.
    d. The hour of the Eskimo and the wolf is over.

Julie Multiple Choice Unit Test 1 Page 6

III. Vocabulary

___ 1. HOISTED   a. set up

___ 2. DISCERN   b. treeless area between ice cap and tree lines in arctic regions

___ 3. ERECTED   c. mourning

___ 4. DEFT   d. following a winding course

___ 5. MENACINGLY   e. to surmise to be true or probable

___ 6. CONVENIENCE   f. small piece or bite of food

___ 7. CRESCENDO   g. able to be handled or controlled

___ 8. TUNDRA   h. raised up; lifted up

___ 9. PONDERED   i. considered carefully

___ 10. PITEOUSLY   j. wearisome sameness

___ 11. MONOTONY   k. the condition of being temporarily set aside

___ 12. MORSEL   l. troubling

___ 13. ABEYANCE   m. threateningly

___ 14. MEANDERING   n. anything that makes work less difficult

___ 15. DISQUIETING   o. formations of stars

___ 16. INTIMATED   p. skillful

___ 17. SUSPECTED   q. to perceive something obscure or concealed

___ 18. MANAGEABLE   r. pathetically

___ 19. CONSTELLATIONS   s. gradual increase in volume

___ 20. GRIEVING   t. discouraged or inhibited by or as if by threats

MULTIPLE CHOICE UNIT TEST 2 - *Julie of the Wolves*

I. Matching

___ 1. Amaroq   A. Kapugen's new home village

___ 2. Julie   B. Pen pal

___ 3. George   C. Miyax

___ 4. Amy   D. Leader of the pack

___ 5. Ulo   E. Author

___ 6. Kapugen   F. Non-Eskimo Americans

___ 7. Naka   G. Miyax's husband

___ 8. Jello   H. Kapugen's serious partner

___ 9. Tornait   I. Coward; Amaroq killed him

___ 10. Kapu   J. Hunter trained by Kapugen

___ 11. Kangik   K. Knife

___ 12. Martha   L. Miyax's aunt

___ 13. Gussaks   M. Plover

___ 14. Atik   N. Miyax's father

___ 15. Daniel   O. New leader of the pack

Julie Multiple Choice Unit Test 2 Page 2

II. Multiple Choice

1. What happened to Miyax's father?
    a. He paddled his kayak into the Bering Sea and disappeared.
    b. He died of old age.
    c. He got lost on a hunting trip.
    d. He had a sledding accident.

2. How did the author describe Miyax?
    a. "Ttomboy-ish"
    b. "Pclassic Eskimo beauty"
    c. "Ppretty but rugged"
    d. "Hhealthy and natural"

3. Why did Miyax speak half in English and half Eskimo when she said, "Amaroq, Daya, wolf, my friend"?
    a. She was delirious.
    b. Since she was going to San Francisco, she wanted to practice English.
    c. She was hoping he would understand some part of the two languages she knew.
    d. She naturally spoke both languages.

4. To where did Miyax intend to walk?
    a. San Francisco
    b. Point Hope
    c. Nunivak Island
    d. Barrow, Alaska

5. How did Miyax know the direction to Fairbanks?
    a. She saw the skyline of the city on the horizon.
    b. She used her maps.
    c. She calculated the direction based on the location of the North Star.
    d. She saw a plane flying over and assumed it was going to Fairbanks.

6. Why did the hunters return the bladders to the seals?
    a. So the spirits could enter the bodies of the newborn seals
    b. Nno particular reason; they just did
    c. So they wouldn't be wasted
    d. So they could be used again

Julie Multiple Choice Unit Test 2 Page 3

7. How did Miyax react when Kapugen called her Julie?
    a. She didn't care.
    b. She preferred to be called Julie.
    c. She got angry.
    d. She winked at him.

8. How could Miyax get away from Aunt Martha if she wanted to?
    a. She could go work for Nusan.
    b. She could marry Daniel.
    c. She could board at school.
    d. She could spend her vacations with her father.

9. What did Miyax think of Daniel upon meeting him?
    a. She liked him well enough and though he'd make a good husband.
    b. She fell instantly in love with him.
    c. She was disappointed.
    d. She thought he was a slob.

10. What was Kapugen's saying about fear?
    a. Fear is an enemy only in your mind.
    b. If you are afraid, close your eyes and think a happy thought.
    c. Rational thought conquers fear.
    d. When fear seizes, change what you are doing because you are doing something wrong.

11. What was Pearl to tell Nusan?
    a. She saw Julie going out on the ice.
    b. She saw Julie headed towards Judith's house.
    c. She saw Julie headed back to Aunt Martha's house.
    d. She saw Julie trying to kill herself.

12. How did Jello die?
    a. Amaroq killed him.
    b. Miyax killed him.
    c. Hunters killed him.
    d. Kapugen killed him.

Julie Multiple Choice Unit Test 2 Page 4

13. What did the fact that she saw a skua tell Miyax?
    a. Caribou were near.
    b. She was getting closer to the ocean.
    c. Spring had come.
    d. Other people had recently been there.

14. What did bounties encourage?
    a. Fighting among the Eskimos
    b. Killing for money instead of need
    c. Settlers
    d. Farmers

15. What happened to Amaroq?
    a. He drowned after falling through thin ice.
    b. Kapu killed him.
    c. He starved to death.
    d. Hunters killed him.

16. What problem did Amaroq's death cause for the wolf pack?
    a. They were all going their separate ways.
    b. They were fighting among themselves and killed each other off.
    c. They were starving without a leader.
    d. They weren't sleeping and were becoming vicious.

17. Why did Miyax move her pack to the river?
    a. There were no hunters at the river.
    b. Miyax wanted to follow the river to Point Hope.
    c. The pack needed fresh water.
    d. There were more animals to kill for food at the river.

18. Why did Miyax leave her father?
    a. She wanted the old Eskimo life which her father could not offer her.
    b. She wanted to live in San Francisco.
    c. She felt odd living with her father and another woman.
    d. All of the above

20. To what realization does Miyax come?
    a. She will be alone the rest of her life.
    b. The hour of the Eskimo and the wolf is over.
    c. The wolves are her only family now.
    d. Her father doesn't love her.

Julie Multiple Choice Unit Test 2 Page 6

IV. Vocabulary

___ 1. LOWLY a. suited for a low rank; meek; humble

___ 2. MANAGEABLE b. maintain; prolong, keep in existence

___ 3. DISCERN c. irresistible attraction

___ 4. ABEYANCE d. invented without preparation or rehearsal

___ 5. IMMENSE e. called together

___ 6. IMPROVISED f. accompanied to give guidance or protection

___ 7. VERSATILE g. grabs hold of

___ 8. MENACINGLY h. having many uses

___ 9. ESCORTED i. wearisome sameness

___ 10. CRESCENDO j. to perceive something obscure or concealed

___ 11. HOISTED k. treeless area between ice cap and tree lines in arctic regions

___ 12. CONSTELLATIONS l. raised up; lifted up

___ 13. FASCINATION m. huge

___ 14. WEIRS n. threateningly

___ 15. MONOTONY o. formations of stars

___ 16. TUNDRA p. able to be handled or controlled

___ 17. SEIZES q. gradual increase in volume

___ 18. ABUNDANT r. in plentiful supply

___ 19. SUMMONED s. the condition of being temporarily set aside

___ 20. SUSTAIN t. fences put in a stream to catch fish or divert water

ANSWER SHEET FOR MULTIPLE CHOICE UNIT TESTS
Julie of the Wolves

I. Matching

1. ___
2. ___
3. ___
4. ___
5. ___
6. ___
7. ___
8. ___
9. ___
10. ___
11. ___
12. ___
13. ___
14. ___
15. ___

II. Multiple Choice

1. (A) (B) (C) (D)
2. (A) (B) (C) (D)
3. (A) (B) (C) (D)
4. (A) (B) (C) (D)
5. (A) (B) (C) (D)
6. (A) (B) (C) (D)
7. (A) (B) (C) (D)
8. (A) (B) (C) (D)
9. (A) (B) (C) (D)
10. (A) (B) (C) (D)
11. (A) (B) (C) (D)
12. (A) (B) (C) (D)
13. (A) (B) (C) (D)
14. (A) (B) (C) (D)
15. (A) (B) (C) (D)
16. (A) (B) (C) (D)
17. (A) (B) (C) (D)
18. (A) (B) (C) (D)
19. (A) (B) (C) (D)

III. Vocabulary

1. ___
2. ___
3. ___
4. ___
5. ___
6. ___
7. ___
8. ___
9. ___
10. ___
11. ___
12. ___
13. ___
14. ___
15. ___
16. ___
17. ___
18. ___
19. ___
20. ___

ANSWER KEY FOR MULTIPLE CHOICE UNIT TEST 1
Julie of the Wolves

I. Matching	II. Multiple Choice	III. Vocabulary
1. F	1. (A) ( ) (C) (D)	1. H
2. K	2. (A) (B) (C) ( )	2. Q
3. A	3. ( ) (B) (C) (D)	3. A
4. H	4. (A) ( ) (C) (D)	4. P
5. C	5. (A) (B) ( ) (D)	5. M
6. N	6. (A) (B) ( ) (D)	6. N
7. B	7. (A) (B) (C) ( )	7. S
8. D	8. ( ) (B) (C) (D)	8. B
9. M	9. (A) (B) (C) ( )	9. I
10. G	10. (A) (B) ( ) (D)	10. R
11. E	11. (A) ( ) (C) (D)	11. J
12. O	12. (A) ( ) (C) (D)	12. F
13. I	13. ( ) (B) (C) (D)	13. K
14. J	14. (A) (B) ( ) (D)	14. D
15. L	15. (A) (B) (C) ( )	15. L
	16. (A) (B) ( ) (D)	16. T
	17. ( ) (B) (C) (D)	17. E
	18. (A) (B) ( ) (D)	18. G
	19. (A) (B) (C) ( )	19. O
		20. C

ANSWER KEY FOR MULTIPLE CHOICE UNIT TEST 2
Julie of the Wolves

I. Matching	II. Multiple Choice	III. Vocabulary
1. D	1. ( ) (B) (C) (D)	1. A
2. C	2. (A) ( ) (C) (D)	2. P
3. E	3. (A) (B) ( ) (D)	3. J
4. B	4. (A) ( ) (C) (D)	4. S
5. K	5. (A) (B) (C) ( )	5. M
6. N	6. ( ) (B) (C) (D)	6. D
7. H	7. (A) (B) ( ) (D)	7. H
8. I	8. (A) ( ) (C) (D)	8. N
9. M	9. (A) (B) ( ) (D)	9. F
10. O	10. (A) (B) (C) ( )	10. Q
11. A	11. ( ) (B) (C) (D)	11. L
12. L	12. ( ) (B) (C) (D)	12. O
13. F	13. (A) ( ) (C) (D)	13. C
14. J	14. (A) ( ) (C) (D)	14. T
15. G	15. (A) (B) (C) ( )	15. I
	16. (A) (B) ( ) (D)	16. K
	17. (A) (B) (C) ( )	17. G
	18. ( ) (B) (C) (D)	18. R
	19. (A) ( ) (C) (D)	19. E
		20. B

UNIT RESOURCE MATERIALS

BULLETIN BOARD IDEAS - *Julie of the Wolves*

1. Save one corner of the board for the best of students' *Julie of the Wolves* writing assignments.

2. To a travel bulletin board about Alaska, or split a travel board between Alaska and San Francisco (or California).

3. Make a bulletin board about survival skills including pictures illustrating your points.

4. Take one of the word search puzzles from the extra activities section and with a marker copy it over in a large size on the bulletin board. Write the clue words to find to one side. Invite students prior to and after class to find the words and circle them on the bulletin board.

5. Do a bulletin board about careers in the wilderness: game warden, park manager, wildlife conservationist, veterinarian, forest ranger, etc.

6. Make a bulletin board about the Eskimos and their way of life.

7. Post a map of Alaska and/or North America to illustrate the distance between San Francisco and Alaska.

8. Make a bulletin board about wolves showing the areas where they still exist and giving information about their habits.

9. Make a bulletin board about wildlife and wilderness conservation.

EXTRA ACTIVITIES - *Julie of the wolves*

One of the difficulties in teaching a novel is that all students don't read at the same speed. One student who likes to read may take the book home and finish it in a day or two. Sometimes a few students finish the in-class assignments early. The problem, then, is finding suitable extra activities for students.

One thing you can do is to keep a little library in the classroom. For this unit on *Julie of the Wolves*, you might check out from the school library other books by Jean Craighead George. You might also include other related books and articles about wolves, Arctic expeditions, travel in the North, Eskimos, camping, survival skills, or vacationing in Alaska or San Francisco.

Other things you may keep on hand are puzzles. We have made some relating directly to *Julie of the Wolves* for you. Feel free to duplicate them.

Some students may like to draw. You might devise a contest or allow some extra-credit grade for students who draw characters or scenes from *Julie of the Wolves*. Note, too, that if the students do not want to keep their drawings you may pick up some extra bulletin board materials this way. If you have a contest and you supply the prize (a CD or something like that perhaps), you could, possibly, make the drawing itself a non-refundable entry fee.

The pages which follow contain games, puzzles and worksheets. The keys, when appropriate, immediately follow the puzzle or worksheet. There are two main groups of activities: one group for the unit; that is, generally relating to the text, and another group of activities related strictly to the vocabulary.

Directions for these games, puzzles and worksheets are self-explanatory. The object here is to provide you with extra materials you may use in any way you choose.

MORE ACTIVITIES - *Julie of the Wolves*

1. Have students design a book cover (front and back and inside flaps) for *Julie of the Wolves*.

2. Have students design a bulletin board (ready to be put up; not just sketched) for *Julie of the Wolves*.

3. Use some of the related topics (noted earlier for an in-class library) as topics for research, reports, or written papers, or as topics for guest speakers.

4. Take some students camping as a reward for whatever criteria you set. Try to make your criteria so that any student could possibly win the trip.

5. Have an Alaska Day during which you learn about the state of Alaska. This could be done in a number of ways. One way would be to divide your class into groups, one each for climate, history, sites of interest, the people and their customs, clothing, food, etc. Give students a day or two to get their information together and then have all the reports on one day . Perhaps you could require students to include a visual aid. That would add interest to the reports. PBS had a wonderful show on Alaska a few years ago; you might look into showing that as well.

6. Write to another school in another state and see if there is an English class of students who would like to be pen pals for your students.

7. Discuss family traditions -- things your students' families do for holidays, birthdays, vacations, or other special occasions.

8. Take one class period to talk about improvising; ways we "make do" when exactly what we want or need is not available. You could have students write down or tell about times they have had to improvise. Discuss the importance of being able to improvise--to make do--to be able to be flexible.

WORD SEARCH - *Julie of the Wolves*

All words in this list are associated with *Julie of the Wolves*. The words are placed backwards, forward, diagonally, up and down. The included words are listed below the word searches.

```
W C Y S P L C Z G G X K S M R X G F F R S D P T
F Q L R H J L A T F W D C E R W K G X M K M W C
Q F K P Z Q J F R K C D N O S V P J Y W U T K L
F T C S B I B S S I I O Y A L E B A H Y O R Y D
K K B O U N T I E S B T R A I L R G R O W L D Z
T V L C M A R U A Q A O A L A L O E V K A N F O
R U S J R P V K O I T X U D S M S P V E A K C N
X N E G U P A K L E J J D K A P U Y S L A S C G
V Y W S E N T S P R T E H A Z F J C S Y I B T W
F T S A K V K O S B R I D B N D M I A C Z S J L
P K R J X I H K C G W A H S C I K K N V Z H J S
A L P J L E M M I N G S M W Z A E A N U S A N K
S M K G U G D O G S N R J Y V T R L H M J F S M
T S A A F D Y J S C P S V I G F L J G T P L B T
B S F R N H I C G W K U N J N Q A S N M R X I Q
J E L L O G S T P C Y U C A L K C A P M N A J F
Z J N N Y Q I Q H Y N H S K S F D Q Z X N L M F
W X N A S S Q K L R I H B A C V M M W R N V R M
R B S Q L V Z Q M N N F L B P Z F G O Y X R R P
S K X H F P V S Z C M A F T F R F T S H W B L W
```

ALASKA	ESKIMOS	MARTHA	SILVER
AMAROQ	GROWL	NAILS	STAR
AMY	HOPE	NAKA	TAIL
ATIK	JELLO	NUNIVAKISLAND	TORNAIT
BLADDER	JUDITH	NUSAN	TRAIL
BONE	JULIE	PACK	ULO
BOUNTIES	KANGIK	PARKAS	UMA
CARIBOU	KAPU	PEARL	WHITEOUT
CHIN	KAPUGEN	PLANE	WOLF
COMPASS	KAYAK	POLLOCK	ZIT
DANIEL	KISPUCK	SANFRANCISCO	
DRUM	LEMMINGS	SEAL	

KEY: WORD SEARCH - *Julie of the Wolves*

All words in this list are associated with *Julie of the Wolves*. The words are placed backwards, forward, diagonally, up and down. The included words are listed below the word searches.

```
                    C           K
                  A           C E              M
                Z     R K    N O     P       W U
              C   I S   I I O  A L E B A       O R
            B O U N T I E S B T R A I L R G R O W L D
              L  M A   U A   A O A L A O E   K A N F O
          U      R P   K O I   U D   M S P V E A K   C
          N E G U P A K L E   J D K A P U     S L A S
              S E N   S P   T E   A         S Y I
              A K     O S   R I   N       I A C   S
          R     I H K       A H     I K K N
        A L  J L E M M I N G S M W   A E A N U S A N
        M K  U   O   S       Y V   R L H
           A  A D   S     P     I   F       T       T
              R N   I       U N   N   A       R     I
         J E L L O G   T     U C A   K C A P     A
              N   Q I   H   N H S K S         N   M
              A     K     I     A             R
              L         N       L           O
              P         A                 T
```

ALASKA	ESKIMOS	MARTHA	SILVER
AMAROQ	GROWL	NAILS	STAR
AMY	HOPE	NAKA	TAIL
ATIK	JELLO	NUNIVAKISLAND	TORNAIT
BLADDER	JUDITH	NUSAN	TRAIL
BONE	JULIE	PACK	ULO
BOUNTIES	KANGIK	PARKAS	UMA
CARIBOU	KAPU	PEARL	WHITEOUT
CHIN	KAPUGEN	PLANE	WOLF
COMPASS	KAYAK	POLLOCK	ZIT
DANIEL	KISPUCK	SANFRANCISCO	
DRUM	LEMMINGS	SEAL	

CROSSWORD - *Julie of the Wolves*

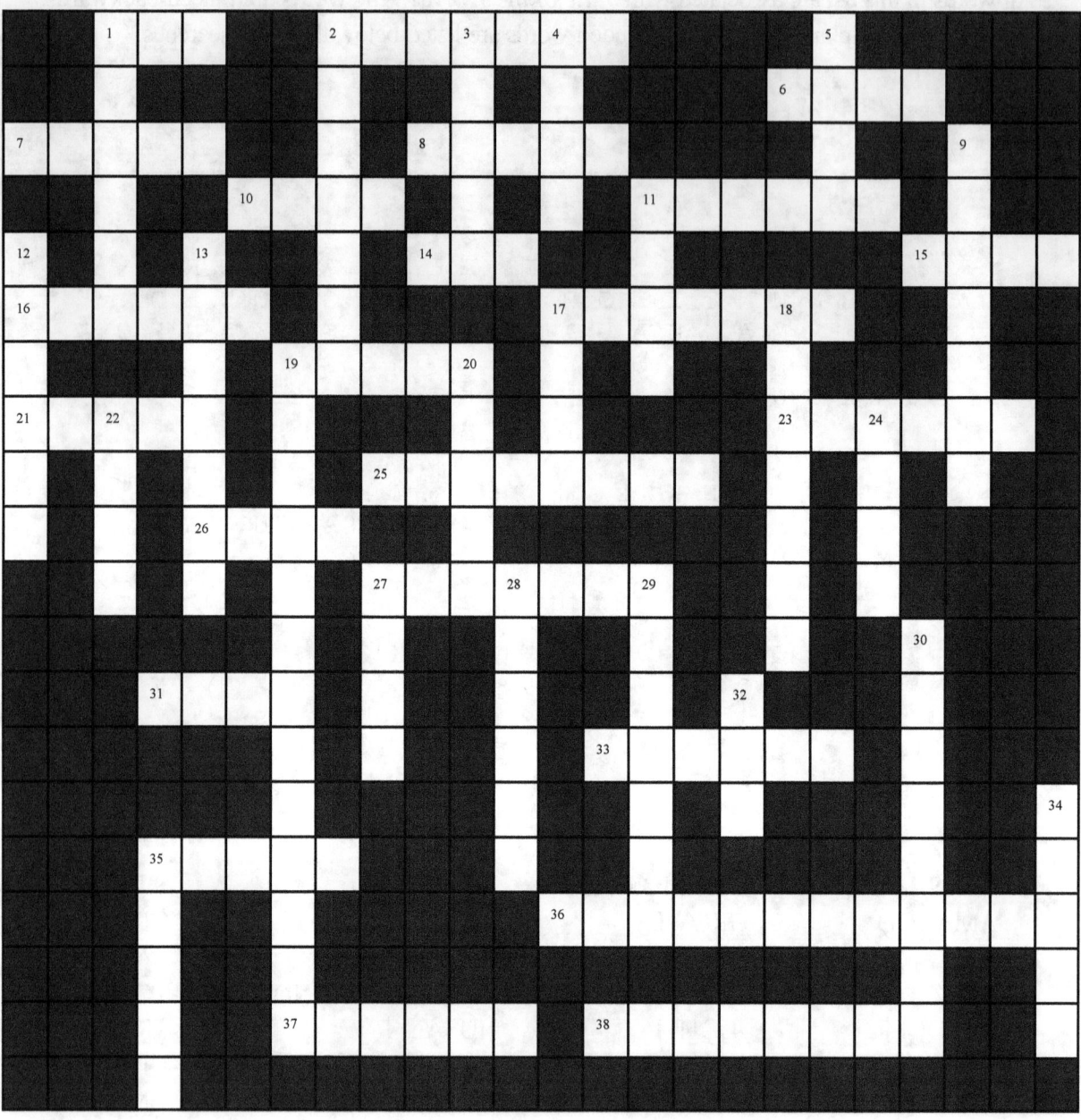

CROSSWORD CLUES - *Julie of the Wolves*

ACROSS
1. Julie's pen pal
2. Instrument for detecting direction
6. Jello, for example
7. Hunters flying in one killed Amaroq
8. Kapugen left in his; small boat
10. Wolf anatomy that sometimes wags to communicate; opposite of head
11. Mother wolf
14. Woman's versatile tool
15. Miyax hid in one for safety from the plane
16. Miyax's special wolf-friend, the leader
17. These bags kept clothes dry at night
19. She makes parkas and mittens for tourists
21. Miyax left one to find her way back
23. Kapugen's new home town
25. Snow coming down so thickly one can't see through it
26. Place a wolf bites to express love
27. Summer dress
31. A group of dogs that live together
33. Talks back to her parents and doesn't follow Eskimo ways
35. He stole Miyax's food - goods
36. Amy's hometown
37. Naka's son, Miyax's husband
38. The hour of the _____

DOWN
1. State where Eskimo's live
2. Meat on the hoof for Miyax
3. She gave Miyax food, a sleeping skin and a ground cloth
4. Kind of camp Kapugen lived in
5. Point _____; Miyax's destination to meet the ship
9. Miyax's plover pet
11. The North _____; name of the ship Miyax hoped to meet
12. Miyax's aunt
13. Amy's father's last name
17. Raw material for making combs, weapons and utensils
18. Miyax's race of people
19. Place of Miyax's birth
20. The grey wolf
22. Hunter who visits Miyax
24. He drank too much
27. New leader of the pack after Amaroq died
28. Nusan made them for tourists
29. Miyax's father
30. Encouraged killing for money instead of need
32. Zat's sibling
34. Throaty wolf communication
35. Miyax

CROSSWORD ANSWER KEY - *Julie of the Wolves*

MATCHING QUIZ/WORKSHEET 1 - Julie of the Wolves

___ 1. JELLO   A. Hunters flying in one killed Amaroq
___ 2. NUNIVAKISLAND   B. She makes parkas and mittens for tourists.
___ 3. KAPU   C. Julie's pen pal
___ 4. KISPUCK   D. State where Eskimo's live
___ 5. JULIE   E. Miyax's aunt
___ 6. TORNAIT   F. Summer dress
___ 7. AMAROQ   G. Woman's versitle tool
___ 8. AMY   H. Place of Miyax's birth
___ 9. ULO   I. Zat's sibling
___10. PLANE   J. Meat on the hoof for Miyax
___11. ALASKA   K. Miyax's father
___12. NUSAN   L. Mother wolf
___13. GROWL   M. Miyax's race of people
___14. SILVER   N. She gave Miyax food, a sleeping skin and a ground cloth.
___15. CARIBOU   O. New leader of the pack after Amaroq died
___16. MARTHA   P. He drank too much.
___17. MIYAX   Q. He stole Miyax's food & goods.
___18. UMA   R. Throaty wolf communication
___19. PEARL   S. Instrument for detecting direction
___20. NAKA   T. Atik's wife
___21. STAR   U. Julie
___22. ESKIMOS   V. The North _____; name of the ship Miyax hoped to meet
___23. COMPASS   W. Miyax
___24. ZIT   X. Miyax's plover pet
___25. KAPUGEN   Y. Miyax's special wolf-friend, the leader

KEY: MATCHING QUIZ/WORKSHEET 1 - Julie of the Wolves

Q - 1.	JELLO	A.	Hunters flying in one killed Amaroq
H - 2.	NUNIVAKISLAND	B.	She makes parkas and mittens for tourists.
O - 3.	KAPU	C.	Julie's pen pal
F - 4.	KISPUCK	D.	State where Eskimo's live
W 5.	JULIE	E.	Miyax's aunt
X - 6.	TORNAIT	F.	Summer dress
Y - 7.	AMAROQ	G.	Woman's versitle tool
C - 8.	AMY	H.	Place of Miyax's birth
G - 9.	ULO	I.	Zat's sibling
A -10.	PLANE	J.	Meat on the hoof for Miyax
D -11.	ALASKA	K.	Miyax's father
B -12.	NUSAN	L.	Mother wolf
R -13.	GROWL	M.	Miyax's race of people
L -14.	SILVER	N.	She gave Miyax food, a sleeping skin and a ground cloth.
J - 15.	CARIBOU	O.	New leader of the pack after Amaroq died
E -16.	MARTHA	P.	He drank too much.
U -17.	MIYAX	Q.	He stole Miyax's food & goods.
T -18.	UMA	R.	Throaty wolf communication
N -19.	PEARL	S.	Instrument for detecting direction
P -20.	NAKA	T.	Atik's wife
V -21.	STAR	U.	Julie
M 22.	ESKIMOS	V.	The North _____; name of the ship Miyax hoped to meet
S -23.	COMPASS	W.	Miyax
I - 24.	ZIT	X.	Miyax's plover pet
K -25.	KAPUGEN	Y.	Miyax's special wolf-friend, the leader

MATCHING QUIZ/WORKSHEET 2 - Julie of the Wolves

___ 1. MIYAX   A. Jello, for example

___ 2. CHIN   B. She gave Miyax food, a sleeping skin and a ground cloth.

___ 3. NAKA   C. Amy's hometown: San ___

___ 4. KAPU   D. Amy's father's last name

___ 5. WHITEOUT   E. Talks back to her parents and doesn't follow Eskimo ways

___ 6. DANIEL   F. Snow coming down so thickly one can't see through it

___ 7. MARTHA   G. Miyax hid in one for safety from the plane.

___ 8. KISPUCK   H. Zat's sibling

___ 9. JUDITH   I. Place of Miyax's birth

___10. TORNAIT   J. State where Eskimo's live

___11. AMAROQ   K. She makes parkas and mittens for tourists.

___12. POLLOCK   L. Miyax's aunt

___13. KAYAK   M. The grey wolf

___14. NUSAN   N. New leader of the pack after Amaroq died

___15. NUNIVAKISLAND   O. Miyax left one to find her way back.

___16. BONE   P. He drank too much.

___17. UMA   Q. Naka's son, Miyax's husband

___18. NAILS   R. Kapugen left in his; small boat

___19. ALASKA   S. Raw material for making combs, weapons and utensils

___20. PEARL   T. Place a wolf bites to express love

___21. WOLF   U. Summer dress

___22. FRANCISCO   V. Miyax's special wolf-friend, the leader

___23. DRUM   W. Miyax's plover pet

___24. TRAIL   X. Julie

___25. ZIT   Y. Atik's wife

KEY: MATCHING QUIZ/WORKSHEET 2 - Julie of the Wolves

X - 1. MIYAX		A. Jello, for example
T - 2. CHIN		B. She gave Miyax food, a sleeping skin and a ground cloth.
P - 3. NAKA		C. Amy's hometown: San ___
N - 4. KAPU		D. Amy's father's last name
F - 5. WHITEOUT		E. Talks back to her parents and doesn't follow Eskimo ways
Q - 6. DANIEL		F. Snow coming down so thickly one can't see through it
L - 7. MARTHA		G. Miyax hid in one for safety from the plane.
U - 8. KISPUCK		H. Zat's sibling
E - 9. JUDITH		I. Place of Miyax's birth
W 10. TORNAIT		J. State where Eskimo's live
V -11. AMAROQ		K. She makes parkas and mittens for tourists.
D -12. POLLOCK		L. Miyax's aunt
R -13. KAYAK		M. The grey wolf
K -14. NUSAN		N. New leader of the pack after Amaroq died
I - 15. NUNIVAKISLAND		O. Miyax left one to find her way back.
S -16. BONE		P. He drank too much.
Y -17. UMA		Q. Naka's son, Miyax's husband
M ·18. NAILS		R. Kapugen left in his; small boat
J - 19. ALASKA		S. Raw material for making combs, weapons and utensils
B -20. PEARL		T. Place a wolf bites to express love
A -21. WOLF		U. Summer dress
C -22. FRANCISCO		V. Miyax's special wolf-friend, the leader
G -23. DRUM		W. Miyax's plover pet
O -24. TRAIL		X. Julie
H -25. ZIT		Y. Atik's wife

JUGGLE LETTER REVIEW GAME CLUES - *Julie of the Wolves*

CLUE	WORD	DEFINITION
OUL	ULO	Woman's versatile tool
ILTA	TAIL	Wagging wolf anatomy; opposite of head
KUKCSPI	KISPUCK	Summer dress
UBAOIRC	CARIBOU	Meat on the hoof for Julie
LSNIA	NAILS	The grey wolf
AMTARH	MARTHA	Miyax's aunt
ALES	SEAL	Kind of camp Kapugen lived in
ANAK	NAKA	He drank too much
LAPEN	LANE	Hunters flying in one killed Amaroq
ENBO	BONE	Raw material for making combs, weapons and utensils
IOSESKM	ESKIMOS	Miyax's race of people
AYKKA	KAYAK	Kapugen left in his; small boat
TKAI	ATIK	Hunter who visits Miyax
DEDLARB	BLADDER	These bags kept clothes dry at night
RTNAINOT	TORNAIT	Miyax's plover pet
MAU	UMA	Atik's wife
GSIMELMN	LEMMINGS	The hour of the ___
AMSOSCP	COMPASS	Instrument for detecting direction
QOMAAR	AMAROQ	Miyax's special wolf-friend; the leader
ROWLG	GROWL	Throaty wolf communications
EIJUL	JULIE	Miyax
AIKNGK	KANGIK	Kapugen's new home town
PEOH	HOPE	Point ___
MYA	AMY	Julie's pen pal
TZI	ZIT	Zat's sibling
HNCI	CHIN	Place a wolf bites to express love
ACKP	PACK	A group of dogs that live together
OUBENSTI	BOUNTIES	They encouraged killing for money instead of need
USANN	NUSAN	She makes parkas and mittens for the tourists
TW HIOTEU	WHITE OUT	Snow coming down so thickly one can't see through it
ILRAT	TRAIL	Miyax left one to find her way back
FISSCCNAOANR	SAN FRANCISCO	Amy's hometown
MDRU	DRUM	Miyax hid in one for safety from the plane
EDALIN	DANIEL	Naka's son; Miyax's husband

VOCABULARY RESOURCE MATERIALS

VOCABULARY WORD SEARCH - *Julie of the Wolves*

All words in this list are associated with the vocabulary from *Julie of the Wolves*. The words are placed backwards, forward, diagonally, up and down. The included words are listed below the word searches.

```
P O N D E R E D E T S I O H G R I E V I N G G S
T K E F I S N C P Y D D S M Z F L D C I S N W S
P W J C N S R L N R N G G C Y B W W A L I Y T V
A P R E D I C A M E N T C X A T X T V G I D W Y
Z P M H H B W E C I I M W E V D S Z A S Q P R B
B M D Y D H B S R D E N G Y E U F R N N D I S T
I L O W L Y E E J N I A E S S L O O X M U M J E
K L G K J R D B A Z N S I V B F I G Q Q C M H N
F G H G C N I C L A F V Q D N T W F N V G N X Y
W A F V A N I N M C O H E U A O J I X K P J L D
D K S E X N M G T R D T J L I A C F J I T K Q V
H E M C G T C O P I R E L V X E B S T C K L H J
L F T L I F V M N O M E N F I R T E X K L E M A
W F Y C R N I Y C O T I X O A T O I Y F N Y B E
S C W Q E L A S D S T Q D R M U A D N A L U R V
R E C T E P E T N G Y O D A S M W L M G N E G P
B J Z S B H S O I Q S N N L T X U O I D C C H D
W X R I D I C U L O U S Y Y V E R S A T I L E P
Z O N J E C Z I S T N Z N L C E D N E D Y F P B
M W E I R S Y E N G U L F E D F T D Q R T S Z V
```

ABEYANCE	ENGULFED	LOWLY	SEIZES
ABUNDANT	ERECTED	MANAGEABLE	SUMMONED
AWED	ESCORTED	MEANDERING	SUSPECTED
CONSTELLATIONS	FASCINATION	MENACINGLY	SUSTAIN
CONVENIENCE	FORAGING	MONOTONY	TUNDRA
CRESCENDO	GRIEVING	MORSEL	VERSATILE
DEFT	HOISTED	NICHE	VITALITY
DISCERN	IMMENSE	PITEOUSLY	WEIRS
DISQUIETING	IMPROVISED	PONDERED	
ECLIPSE	INQUIRY	PREDICAMENT	
ENAMORED	INTIMIDATED	RIDICULOUS	

KEY: VOCABULARY WORD SEARCH - *Julie of the Wolves*

All words in this list are associated with the vocabulary from *Julie of the Wolves*. The words are placed backwards, forward, diagonally, up and down. The included words are listed below the word searches.

```
            P O N D E R E D E T S I O H G R I E V I N G G
              E   I S   C       D           L   C   I   N
              W   N S   N   N G       B       A L I
            A P R E D I C A M E N T       A   T   G I       Y
                M           E C I I M   E   D S   A S   P R
                M           S R D E N G   E U   R N     I S
            I L O W L Y E E   N I A E S S   O O     U   E
                      R D   A   N S I V   F I     Q
            F       C N I C   A   V Q D N T       N
                A     A   I N M   O   E U A O   I     P
            D   S E   N M   T R D T   L I A C         I
                E M C G     O P I R E L V   E B   T
                  T L I     M N O M E N   I T E         E   A
                  Y C   N I   C O T I   O A T O I Y   N   B E
            S       E L A S     S T     D R M U A   N A   U R
                E     E P E T N     O D A S M   L M G N E
                  Z S   H S O I     N N L T   U O I D C C     D
                R I D I C U L O U S Y Y V E R S A T I L E
                O     E     I S T N           E D N E   Y F
            M W E I R S   E N G U L F E D     T D       T
```

ABEYANCE	ENGULFED	LOWLY	SEIZES
ABUNDANT	ERECTED	MANAGEABLE	SUMMONED
AWED	ESCORTED	MEANDERING	SUSPECTED
CONSTELLATIONS	FASCINATION	MENACINGLY	SUSTAIN
CONVENIENCE	FORAGING	MONOTONY	TUNDRA
CRESCENDO	GRIEVING	MORSEL	VERSATILE
DEFT	HOISTED	NICHE	VITALITY
DISCERN	IMMENSE	PITEOUSLY	WEIRS
DISQUIETING	IMPROVISED	PONDERED	
ECLIPSE	INQUIRY	PREDICAMENT	
ENAMORED	INTIMIDATED	RIDICULOUS	

VOCABULARY CROSSWORD - *Julie of the Wolves*

VOCABULARY CROSSWORD CLUES - *Julie of the Wolves*

ACROSS

1. Gradual increase in volume
7. Having an emotion or mixed reverence, dread or wonder
9. Raw material for making combs, weapons and utensils
11. A question
13. Hunter who visits Miyax
14. Maintain; prolong, keep in existence
17. Inspired with love; captivated; charmed
18. Woman's versatile tool
19. The condition of being temporarily set aside
21. Miyax hid in one for safety from the plane
22. A steep, shallow recess in a rock or hill
25. The grey wolf
26. Zat's sibling
30. Small piece or bite of food
32. Grabs hold of
34. Jello, for example
35. Wolf anatomy that sometimes wags to communicate; opposite of head
38. She makes parkas and mittens for tourists
41. Treeless area between ice cap and tree lines in arctic regions
42. Julie's pen pal
43. Vigor, energy
44. These bags kept clothes dry at night

DOWN

2. Absurd; preposterous; laughable
3. Formations of stars
4. Skillful
5. Instrument for detecting direction
6. Having many uses
7. In plentiful supply
8. Anything that makes work less difficult
10. A group of dogs that live together
12. To perceive something obscure or concealed
15. Irresistible attraction
16. Searching for food; rummaging looking for provisions
20. The obscuring of one celestial body by another
23. Huge
24. Raised up; lifted up
27. Mourning
28. Set up
29. Accompanied to give guidance or protection
30. Wearisome sameness
31. Suited for a low rank; meek; humble
33. Hunters flying in one killed Amaroq
36. Kapugen left in his; small boat
37. Kind of camp Kapugen lived in
39. The North _____; name of the ship Miyax hoped to meet
40. He drank too much

VOCABULARY CROSSWORD - *Julie of the Wolves*

VOCABULARY WORKSHEET 1 - Julie of the Wolves

___ 1. VERSATILE   A. Small piece or bite of food
___ 2. MORSEL   B. Having many uses
___ 3. CONSTELLATIONS   C. In plentiful supply
___ 4. INQUIRY   D. Formations of stars
___ 5. PITEOUSLY   E. Threateningly
___ 6. ENAMORED   F. Treeless area between ice cap and tree lines in arctic regions
___ 7. IMMENSE   G. Troublesome situation
___ 8. PREDICAMENT   H. Huge
___ 9. PONDERED   I. Considered carefully
___ 10. AWED   J. Having an emotion or mixed reverence, dread or wonder
___ 11. TUNDRA   K. Surrounded completely
___ 12. ERECTED   L. Inspired with love; captivated; charmed
___ 13. ABUNDANT   M. Accompanied to give guidance or protection
___ 14. FASCINATION   N. Called together
___ 15. ENGULFED   O. The condition of being temporarily set aside
___ 16. WEIRS   P. Discouraged or inhibited by or as if by threats
___ 17. DEFT   Q. Absurd; preposterous; laughable
___ 18. ESCORTED   R. Set up
___ 19. INTIMIDATED   S. Invented without preparation or rehearsal
___ 20. MENACINGLY   T. Anything that makes work less difficult
___ 21. CONVENIENCE   U. Fences put in a stream to catch fish or divert water
___ 22. RIDICULOUS   V. Pathetically
___ 23. SUMMONED   W. Irresistible attraction
___ 24. ABEYANCE   X. Skillful
___ 25. IMPROVISED   Y. A question

KEY: VOCABULARY WORKSHEET 1 - Julie of the Wolves

B - 1.	VERSATILE	A.	Small piece or bite of food
A - 2.	MORSEL	B.	Having many uses
D - 3.	CONSTELLATIONS	C.	In plentiful supply
Y - 4.	INQUIRY	D.	Formations of stars
V - 5.	PITEOUSLY	E.	Threateningly
L - 6.	ENAMORED	F.	Treeless area between ice cap and tree lines in arctic regions
H - 7.	IMMENSE	G.	Troublesome situation
G - 8.	PREDICAMENT	H.	Huge
I - 9.	PONDERED	I.	Considered carefully
J - 10.	AWED	J.	Having an emotion or mixed reverence, dread or wonder
F - 11.	TUNDRA	K.	Surrounded completely
R - 12.	ERECTED	L.	Inspired with love; captivated; charmed
C - 13.	ABUNDANT	M.	Accompanied to give guidance or protection
W - 14.	FASCINATION	N.	Called together
K - 15.	ENGULFED	O.	The condition of being temporarily set aside
U - 16.	WEIRS	P.	Discouraged or inhibited by or as if by threats
X - 17.	DEFT	Q.	Absurd; preposterous; laughable
M - 18.	ESCORTED	R.	Set up
P - 19.	INTIMIDATED	S.	Invented without preparation or rehearsal
E - 20.	MENACINGLY	T.	Anything that makes work less difficult
T - 21.	CONVENIENCE	U.	Fences put in a stream to catch fish or divert water
Q - 22.	RIDICULOUS	V.	Pathetically
N - 23.	SUMMONED	W.	Irresistible attraction
O - 24.	ABEYANCE	X.	Skillful
S - 25.	IMPROVISED	Y.	A question

VOCABULARY WORKSHEET 2 - Julie of the Wolves

___ 1. SUSTAIN   A. Fences put in a stream to catch fish or divert water
___ 2. PREDICAMENT   B. Grabs hold of
___ 3. MORSEL   C. Called together
___ 4. SUMMONED   D. Inspired with love; captivated; charmed
___ 5. MONOTONY   E. Invented without preparation or rehearsal
___ 6. PITEOUSLY   F. Maintain; prolong, keep in existence
___ 7. ABUNDANT   G. Absurd; preposterous; laughable
___ 8. IMPROVISED   H. Following a winding course
___ 9. ENAMORED   I. Wearisome sameness
___10. CRESCENDO   J. Accompanied to give guidance or protection
___11. DISQUIETING   K. Suited for a low rank; meek; humble
___12. LOWLY   L. A steep, shallow recess in a rock or hill
___13. INTIMIDATED   M. A question
___14. NICHE   N. Pathetically
___15. SEIZES   O. Discouraged or inhibited by or as if by threats
___16. RIDICULOUS   P. In plentiful supply
___17. INQUIRY   Q. Small piece or bite of food
___18. WEIRS   R. Gradual increase in volume
___19. VITALITY   S. Treeless area between ice cap and tree lines in arctic regions
___20. TUNDRA   T. Troubling
___21. CONSTELLATIONS   U. Vigor, energy
___22. ESCORTED   V. Raised up; lifted up
___23. MANAGEABLE   W. Troublesome situation
___24. MEANDERING   X. Formations of stars
___25. HOISTED   Y. Able to be handled or controlled

KEY: VOCABULARY WORKSHEET 2 - Julie of the Wolves

F - 1.	SUSTAIN	A. Fences put in a stream to catch fish or divert water
W - 2.	PREDICAMENT	B. Grabs hold of
Q - 3.	MORSEL	C. Called together
C - 4.	SUMMONED	D. Inspired with love; captivated; charmed
I - 5.	MONOTONY	E. Invented without preparation or rehearsal
N - 6.	PITEOUSLY	F. Maintain; prolong, keep in existence
P - 7.	ABUNDANT	G. Absurd; preposterous; laughable
E - 8.	IMPROVISED	H. Following a winding course
D - 9.	ENAMORED	I. Wearisome sameness
R - 10.	CRESCENDO	J. Accompanied to give guidance or protection
T - 11.	DISQUIETING	K. Suited for a low rank; meek; humble
K - 12.	LOWLY	L. A steep, shallow recess in a rock or hill
O - 13.	INTIMIDATED	M. A question
L - 14.	NICHE	N. Pathetically
B - 15.	SEIZES	O. Discouraged or inhibited by or as if by threats
G - 16.	RIDICULOUS	P. In plentiful supply
M - 17.	INQUIRY	Q. Small piece or bite of food
A - 18.	WEIRS	R. Gradual increase in volume
U - 19.	VITALITY	S. Treeless area between ice cap and tree lines in arctic regions
S - 20.	TUNDRA	T. Troubling
X - 21.	CONSTELLATIONS	U. Vigor, energy
J - 22.	ESCORTED	V. Raised up; lifted up
Y - 23.	MANAGEABLE	W. Troublesome situation
H - 24.	MEANDERING	X. Formations of stars
V - 25.	HOISTED	Y. Able to be handled or controlled

VOCABULARY JUGGLE LETTER REVIEW GAME CLUES - *Julie of the Wolves*

1.	DLFEFEUN	ENGULFED	surrounded, completed
2.	COLIIUSDUR	RIDICULOUS	absurd; preposterous; laughable
3.	GIFRAOGN	FORAGING	searching for food; rummaging; looking for provisions
4.	NQUIYIR	INQUIRY	a question
5.	ITVYTLIA	VITALITY	vigor, energy
6.	UOPYIELST	PITEOUSLY	pathetically
7.	NNABTADU	ABUNDANT	in plentiful supply
8.	NMSUEODM	SUMMONED	called together
9.	LSOERM	MORSEL	small piece or bite of food
10.	MDIINATIDTE	INTIMIDATED	discouraged or inhibited by or as if by threats
11.	IDGSNIQUETI	DISQUIETING	troubling
12.	YNOOMNTO	MONOTONY	wearisome sameness
13.	EDCCNOSRE	CRESCENDO	gradual increase in volume
14.	IEGRNGIV	GRIEVING	mourning
15.	DEWA	AWED	having an emotion or mixed reverence, dread or wonder
16.	MEIMENS	IMMENSE	huge
17.	ESRIW	WEIRS	fences put in a stream to catch fish or divert water
18.	IEZESS	SEIZES	grabs hold of
19.	ALBGAAEENM	MANAGEABLE	able to be handled or controlled
20.	TNUAISS	SUSTAIN	maintain; prolong, keep in existence
21.	PLCEIES	ECLIPSE	the obscuring of one celestial body by another
22.	CETDEER	ERECTED	set up
23.	ULNFDEGE	ENGULFED	surrounded completely
24.	IENCH	NICHE	a steep, shallow recess in a rock or hill
25.	RCIDNES	DISCERN	to perceive something obscure or concealed
26.	YWLOL	LOWLY	suited for a low rank; meek; humble
27.	IDHTEOS	HOISTED	raised up; lifted up
28.	EDENPODR	PONDERED	considered carefully
29.	RIVESDOMIP	IMPROVISED	invented without preparation or rehearsal
30.	LAEVEITSRI	VERSATILE	having many uses
31.	CEECVNNOEIN	CONVENIENCE	anything that makes work less difficult
32.	DSPCEEUTS	SUSPECTED	to surmise to be true or probable
33.	EANCEABY	ABEYANCE	the condition of being temporarily set aside
34.	INYNEAGMCL	MENACINGLY	threateningly
35.	FTED	DEFT	skillful
36.	CESEDORT	ESCORTED	accompanied to give guidance or protection